Yesterday's Los Angeles

Seemann's Historic Cities Series

NORMAN DASH

Yesterday's

LOS ANGELES

Seemann's Historic Cities Series No. 26

E. A. Seemann Publishing, Inc.
Miami, Florida

A great many individuals and institutions kindly supported the author's task of collecting photographs for this book. Their contributions are credited in abbreviated form at the end of each caption. All pictures without credit are from the author's collection; the contributors are the following:

Alcana	Lou Alcana Photo Collection, Los Angeles	LB	Port of Long Beach
American	American Airlines, Los Angeles	Locklear	*Locklear: The Man Who Walked On Wings* by Art Ronnie
Bayrd	Lee Bayrd's *Los Angeles Scenes*	Ormond	John Ormond Photo, Los Angeles
CHB	Cultural Heritage Board, Los Angeles	PER	Pacific Electric Railway, Los Angeles
CHMC	California Hospital Medical Center, Los Angeles	PT	Pacific Telephone, Los Angeles
CSAF	Citizens Savings Athletic Foundation, Los Angeles	Ronnie	The Art Ronnie Collection, Los Angeles
Danning	Neal Danning Pictures, Los Angeles	SART	Santa Anita Race Track, Arcadia
DeMille	Cecil B. DeMille Trust, Los Angeles	SFR	Santa Fe Railway, Los Angeles
Douglas	Douglas Aircraft Company, Los Angeles	Shanfeld	Isaac Shanfeld Historical Pictures, Los Angeles
Firestone	Firestone Tire and Rubber Company, South Gate	Spence	Spence Air Photos, Los Angeles
Fraggi	The Don Fraggi Collection, Los Angeles	SPNB	Security Pacific National Bank, Los Angeles
H-E	*Los Angeles Herald-Examiner*	Title	Title Insurance and Trust Company, Los Angeles
Kyson	Charles Kyson, Beverly Hills	Twentieth	Twentieth Century-Fox Studio, Los Angeles
LACF	Los Angeles County Fair	UCLA	University of California at Los Angeles, Westwood
LACSD	Los Angeles County Sheriff's Department	Universal	Universal Pictures Company, Los Angeles
LADRP	Los Angeles Department of Recreation and Parks	USA	United States Army, Los Angeles
LADWP	Los Angeles Department of Water and Power	USC	University of Southern California, Los Angeles
LAFD	Los Angeles Fire Department	Western	Western Air Lines, Los Angeles
LAHD	Los Angeles Harbor Department	Whitehead	Charles Whitehead, Los Angeles
LAUSD	Los Angeles Unified School District	YMCA	YMCA of Metropolitan Los Angeles

Library of Congress Cataloging in Publication Data

```
Dash, Norman.
    Yesterday's Los Angeles.

    (Seemann's historic cities series ; no. 26)
    Bibliography:  p.
    Includes index.
    1.  Los Angeles--History--Pictorial works.
 2.  Los Angeles--Description--Views.  I.  Title.
F869.L843D37      979.4'94'00222      76-21249
ISBN 0-912458-70-4
```

Copyright © 1976 by Norman Dash
Library of Congress Catalog Card No. 76-21249
ISBN 0-912458-70-4

Manufactured in the United States of America.

To my wife,
Lucille,
who helped with the editing, and to my children, Annette and
Jeffrey, who constantly urged me to finish and get it over with.
Also, my thanks to the countless photographers, who, throughout
history, took the pictures that made this book possible.

Contents

LANDING OF CABRILLO · 1542

JOHN RODRIGUEZ CABRILLO, the discoverer of California, is depicted on canvas as he landed in 1542 at what is now the San Pedro bay area. About ten feet by fifteen feet, this painting by artist Charles H. Davis was part of a WPA federal art project, and hung in the Los Angeles County Hall of Records from 1939 until the building was torn down in 1972.

Preface

SOONER OR LATER someone is going to ask me why I accepted the assignment of putting together *Yesterday's Los Angeles,* one of the city books in the historic series published by the Ernest A. Seemann Publishing company. At first I thought, because I'm a newspaper editor and a feature writer, a book would be easy for me. I figured that I could simply throw the material together and, presto, a book would result. How wrong I was.

Naturally, there were problems, the most difficult being to locate the right kind of pictures. Fortunately, through the *Los Angeles Herald-Examiner* and the Title Insurance and Trust Company, plus many other sources, I found a great many.

In the beginning, I spent days and nights fruitlessly visiting people who had scrapbooks filled with old pictures. Afterwards, with more success, I went through countless public and professional collections until I thought I would never be able to look another picture in the face again. I must have checked out at least twenty-five thousand photographs in an effort to find the more than three hundred which are in this book.

Now, many months after I started, I can honestly look back and say that all the looking and studying and searching was really enjoyable. Also, it was fun traveling to the various libraries to find books about Los Angeles, and to read about another time and another age.

All my life in the newspaper business I've studied photographs of every kind imaginable, but to tell the truth, none have fascinated me as much as these. All my life I've written about people of all kinds and types, some of whom were famous, and of the things they accomplished. Yet, doing so never gave me as much pleasure as when I literally lost myself, so to speak, in the birth of this city. It was as if I had taken a science-fiction time machine and traveled backwards and forwards, going from the discovery of California to the present day metropolis.

Other problems arose later. For example, why choose one photo over another, why one house over another, why one individual over another? What makes someone walking down a street more interesting than the street itself? What makes someone flying more attractive than someone swimming, or someone riding a horse more glamorous than someone riding a bicycle? I had to choose, to make decisions, and, believe me, they were difficult!

Perhaps my experience gained from working on magazines and newspapers helped, or maybe I did it intuitively. I really don't know. The important thing is that I completed the task, and in the process became attached to every photograph I collected.

Even after I sent them off to the publisher, I had doubts, and I thought of other photographs I could have included. Maybe the ones I discarded and kept at home were better, more interesting than those I sent? In any case, now I can only wait and see, and let you decide.

Fortunately, *Yesterday's Los Angeles* isn't a scholarly history of Los Angeles. Simply, it is the story of Los Angeles told with a collection of old, preserved pictures. Through them, you too will be able to visit another age, to go back and see how others struggled to live, and to glimpse life in yesterday's hectic, disillusioning, as well as pleasant times. Although they may have some historical significance, many of the pictures, of course, were chosen for their entertainment value, and many only because they excited and moved me.

Now, as my children had wanted, I'm finished. It is complete. I hope you enjoy the result as much as I enjoyed putting it all together.

April, 1976   Norman Dash

BEFORE THE FOUNDING of Los Angeles in 1781, the area was inhabited by the Yang-Na Indians, who were first come upon by Fray Juan Crespi in 1769. In this diorama, the peaceful and mild-mannered Indians and their huts are shown spread out on a bluff over the Los Angeles River, among cottonwood and sycamore trees, on the site where Union Station and Los Angeles City Hall are located today.

Yesterday's Los Angeles

LOS ANGELES is probably one of a handful of cities throughout the world that was planned for greatness—and, more importantly, succeeded. It was the specific order of King Carlos III of Spain to Felipe de Neve, then the Spanish governor of California, that resulted in the founding of Los Angeles on September 4, 1781.

Neve, while at his headquarters in Monterey, received a message forwarded by the Viceroy of Mexico, that King Carlos commanded Neve to establish a pueblo three leagues, approximately eight miles, westward from Mission San Gabriel. The order triggered thoughts in Neve of when he had ridden from Baja California to Monterey in 1776, and of a spacious valley and the Porciuncula (later the Los Angeles) River he had encountered along the way. Neve recalled the lush green hills and the surrounding flat plains, and envisioned it as being populated one day with families, homes, and farms. He found reassuring the words of Father Juan Crespi, who in 1769 described the area as ". . . well grown with cottonwoods and sycamores, among which ran a beautiful river from the north-northwest. . . . This plain where the river runs is very extensive. . . . It has good land for planting all kinds of grain and such. It has all the requisites for a large settlement."

Armed with these remembrances, Neve complied immediately. The bugler sounded the call, the cavalry began its march, and Neve, in a cloud of dust, left Monterey for Mission San Gabriel in August of 1781.

Arriving at the mission, Governor Neve settled down to wait for the colonists who had been recruited from the Mexican provinces of Sonora and Sinaloa. Later, he would discover that rounding up the volunteers had been a difficult and troublesome task. The prospective settlers had to guarantee that they would remain in the proposed city for at least ten years, a period which at the outset would include extreme hardship. As a result, many of the volunteers turned out to be conscripts chosen from anywhere—corraled, rounded up, and deposited, whether they agreed to it or not, on a difficult, sobering journey to another land. Some of them, naturally, objected, but their cries went unheeded. They were needed for the new city, and that's exactly where they would go.

[11]

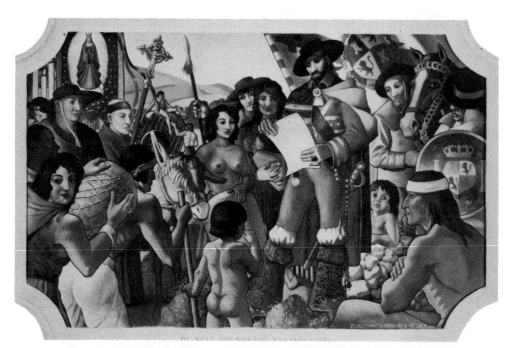

FELIPE DE NEVE, the governor of California, first thought about creating a Los Angeles pueblo at San Gabriel Mission on August 26, 1781. It wasn't until September 4, 1781, however, that the city was actually founded. In this painting by Buckley Mac-Gurran and Ben Messick, which hung in the Los Angeles County Hall of Records from 1939 to 1972, Governor Neve reads the proclamation that outlined the city, established its laws, pinpointed its exact location, and provided for the survey and distribution of lots to colonists.

These first families of Los Angeles were a mixture of Spanish, Negro, and Indian blood, and were really nothing more than poor derelicts and mavericks caught in a situation not of their choosing. They represented the lowest, crudest order of Spanish and Mexican society. They had been gathered to perform the specific function of working the soil and herding the cattle. Nothing more.

Among these early founders were four Indians, one mestizo (half Indian, half Spanish), two Spaniards, two Negroes, and two mulattoes (half Negro, half Spanish), their wives (who were mulattoes or Indians), and twenty-two children, including a newborn baby.

These future colonists were taken to Los Alamos at the Gulf of California. They sailed up the Gulf, and afterwards crossed over bleak, harsh, and desolate country at Velicata in Baja California, from where they marched north to Mission San Gabriel. They finally arrived there on August 18, 1781, about seven and one-half months after they had left Mexico.

Smallpox, however, kept them from immediately leaving the mission for their promised land. Since several children had contracted the disease and were probably not yet quite over it, Governor Neve quarantined everyone until the chance of its spreading had passed.

Soon, on August 26, 1781, while still at Mission San Gabriel, Governor Neve issued his code of laws for the establishment of Los Angeles and prepared the settlers for the short journey to the proposed site. He specified where the city should be located, near a ditch or a river, and pinpointed its traditionally Spanish formation of buildings around a plaza. Neve also decided what acreage the colonists would own, and had the families draw lots for these rectangular pieces of land.

Finally, they were ready. The forty-four colonists, anxious to see their new home, set out with horses and mules along a dusty, old, Indian trail used by the padres whenever they moved north from mission to mission. With the colonists that day were mission representatives, a military escort, and pack animals. Most of the farm animals—cows, sheep, oxen, and goats—were left behind at the mission until such time as they would be needed. The trail they followed meandered between low hills and wild country, and eventually led across the Porciuncula to where the city of Los Angeles was then established.

Since they were alien to the land, the settlers were watched closely by the local Yang-Na Indians, as they wound their way slowly to their remote destination. How they were regarded must remain purely a speculation, because no accounts of the events that transpired were handed down for historians to peruse. With the passing of time, the entire first day's activities, though legend, have become more and more impressive, even angelic to some degree, depending on the story teller.

Lynn Bowman, author of *Los Angeles: Epic of a City*, wrote, "Although the September sun burned fiercely overhead and the land lay faded and parched, wild grapes grew on the opposite shore and rose bushes bloomed. On the bluff over the river, among the cottonwood and sycamore trees, Indians—future neighbors— watched in a friendly manner from their village of Yang-Na. Cool waters flowed by the new home. This was the dry season and the river was shallow, but wide and inviting. Anticipation surged through the group as they gazed, and the line began to advance. Through the water the hooves of the horses splashed. To the delighted shouts and laughter of the children, the journey of the colonists ended."

Approximately on the spot where King Carlos had originally ordered the establishment of the colony, the procession of settlers, the padres from the mission, and their Indian neophytes halted shortly after noon.

His majesty's proclamation was read, a cross was erected, a Te Deum (thanksgiving to God) was sung, musket volleys were fired, plaza boundaries were laid, and stakes were pounded into the ground to mark off lots. When the settlers did pause from their labors, they gazed in awe at their surroundings, and simply stared at the sheltering hills. They could see that they hadn't been misled, that the area definitely would be a good place for a city. Of course, Governor Neve approved. "No streets of it will be swept by the winds," he proclaimed to the large gathering.

Shortly, after a brief rest, the colonists chose the location for a dam and staked out the route of a ditch that would be used to carry water from the river to what would become rich farm lands. Animals, farming utensils, and supplies were left for the settlers, and Governor Neve and the other witnesses to the birth of the city departed, leaving the colonists to their fate in a strange and wild country. Thus, the inhabitants of *el pueblo de la Reina de los Angeles,* the town of the Queen of the Angels, made their beginning.

Five years later, on September 4, 1786, eight of the original settlers and one new-comer took official title to their properties by marking an "X" on their ownership documents; each also received, as originally promised, a registered branding iron for their cattle.

As with all new enterprises, problems developed. Apparently, all was not sweetness and light in the settlement. Shortly after its beginnings, it was discovered that eight of the eleven families were hard-working, good, and conscientious. This description, however, couldn't be applied to the others, and, in fact, they were found to be quite useless. As a result, it was left to Father Junipero Serra, the founder of the missions, on his next visit to Los Angeles, to expel the shirkers.

During this initial year, the pueblo settlers moved cautiously. At first trees, shrubs, and undergrowth had to be cleared away for their home sites, and then shelters had to be constructed for protection against the elements. A year later, the shelters would give way to the more substantial adobes. Concerned with their important living chores, the settlers left the governing of the city to a *comisionado*, Vicente Felix, a Spanish corporal. Felix and five other Mexican soldiers protected the settlers, serving as their leaders until 1788, when Jose Vanegas, an Indian and one of the original founders, was appointed *alcalde*.

Because of its austere location, on a desert hidden by mountains and hills, and its relative inaccessibility to the rest of the world, Los Angeles grew slowly. What population it developed from 1781 to 1791 did little to indicate its future greatness.

The early settlers who did persevere to develop the new land, however, soon learned what the mission fathers already knew: that California soil brought forth a rich source of fruits and grains. This was the lure that helped bring new settlers to the city. More than likely, it hastened the departure from Spanish service its few remaining soldiers, as more and more requests for *ranchos* were made in 1784, only three years after the birth of the city.

Actually, it was the deterioration of the mission system, which had started when Mexico received its independence from Spain, that led to the rise of the huge land grants or ranchos, as they were called by Californians.

Much of the romance of early California days stems from this period in history, and much of what appears on this subject in movies, magazines, books, and art can be directly attributed to the ranchos and their haciendas, corrals, cattle roundups, fiestas, amusements, and the generally free, adventurous and stylish way of living.

J. A. Graves, who spent part of his youth on an early rancho, described the life in his book, *My Seventy Years in California*:

"The native Californians who owned these granted lands led a pastoral life. They lived in a patriarchal manner, sometimes several generations occupying the same family homestead. They had their retainers and followers, many of them full or half-blooded Indians. At the time that Dana made his trip, detailed in *Two Years before the Mast*, and for long afterwards, these people disposed of their hides and tallow to the owners of vessels which beat up and down the coast for cargo. They received largely merchandise of various character and quality for their products. Sometimes a little money changed hands. They led a happy, carefree life. They loved the fiesta and the fandango. They indulged in cock-fighting, horse-racing, and too often they gambled heavily, and many of them drank to

[14]

excess. They were careless of money, spent it freely when they had it, and did not hesitate to borrow when they did not have it. The wives of these old grandees were noble, home-loving women, loyal to their families, and devoted to their religious duties. They tenderly cared for both the physical and spiritual welfare of their children. They pointed out to them the straight and narrow path. They fed and nursed and clothed the Indians, by whom they were surrounded. They restrained the passions and prejudices of their husbands, brothers, and sons, who, too often, were goaded to desperation by the hypocrisy and deception practiced on them by the Americans who were rapidly settling up this country, and who were not over-scrupulous as to the means used in order to attain ends desired."

More than 30 grants were made in what are now Los Angeles and Orange counties during those early years. There was no reason to hold back. The land was so immense, so flowing, and in such depth, that the governors who awarded the grants could afford to be generous. The land was big, dry, and green, and rivers flowed in abundance. Corridors of green followed the rivers to the ocean, and when it was quiet, ocean waves could be heard before they were even seen.

Ranchos were usually measured in square leagues, one of which equalled 4,439 acres. The smallest grant was one quarter of a league, with most being from one to eleven leagues. Grants could be given to anyone at the discretion of whoever was governor. Since it was a time of plenty, each grant was free of charge, with no strings attached. The only requirement was that the person accepting the grant had to construct a house on the property, and had to put out to pasture at least one hundred head of cattle. This was a relatively cheap price to pay for the riches that a land grant brought.

The first request for a land grant was made in 1784 to Gov. Pedro Fages by Manuel Nieto, a Spanish colonel and a favorite of the governor. One of the largest of all grants, about one hundred and fifty thousand acres, Nieto's property ran along the Pacific Ocean between the San Gabriel and the Santa Ana rivers, and rolled northward to the mountains. The sites of today's cities of Long Beach, Whittier, and Anaheim, and much of the area between, were held by Nieto until he died in 1804. Afterwards, it was all divided into smaller ranchos.

The second grant awarded by Governor Fages, also in 1784, went to Jose Maria Verdugo. Called San Rafael Rancho, this grant embraced 36,480 acres lying on the left bank of the Los Angeles River, and extended to the Arroyo Seco. Today, the rancho is the home of Glendale, and parts of Burbank and Pasadena.

Juan Jose Dominguez received the third grant in 1785. Dominguez, an army veteran who had served at the first presidio in San Diego, found himself with 43,179 acres, mostly along the ocean, where now stand the cities of Redondo Beach, Torrance, and Compton, and the community of Wilmington.

Los Angeles residents, however, paid little attention to the dispersal of these huge chunks of land, since life in their own bailiwick was difficult enough. They had their own problems, and it was their own survival which interested them. Who cared about land grants? Obviously, not these harried settlers.

By 1790, there were 20 new citizens, and 29 adobe homes, besides a town hall, a barracks, a guard house, and granaries, all surrounded by an adobe wall. Their stock amounted to 2,418 head, and their crops yielded 4,500 bushels of grain. The population was 139, and in 1793, nine of them were over ninety years old. There was no cloth available from which to make shirts, and prices for livestock, set by Governor Fages, were $5 for an ox or cow, $1 to $2 for sheep, $14 to $20 for a mule, $9 for a well-broken horse, and 25 cents for a chicken.

Ten years later, Los Angeles began spreading out. Historian Charles Dwight Willard wrote, "Los Angeles at the end of the 18th century consisted of about 30 small, adobe houses, 12 of which were clustered around an open square, and the remainder huddled in the vicinity, without much system as to location. The houses were near together, not because land was scarce or valuable, but for sociability and for mutual protection against thieving Indians. Most of the new houses were to the southwest of the plaza, where are now Buena Vista and Castelar streets. To the north and east lay the lower land, and the space reserved for public buildings."

Houses were rickety structures, of one room, with leaky roofs, constructed of poles. Yards, in which cattle were slaughtered, were dirty and unkempt, and were without flowers or shade trees so common today. There was no school, nor did anyone consider educating the young, and Indian labor was so cheap that the settlers had plenty of time for cock fights and music. Residents got drunk, quarrelled, and sometimes fought, but, as a rule, never murdered one another. Foreign vessels were not permitted to visit the coast, so there was very little trade or commerce.

In 1811, the population of Los Angeles jumped to more than five hundred persons, of which ninety-one were heads of families. Willard wrote that "seven were owners of large ranchos or grants in the vicinity of the city; 20 were bona-fide land owners in the pueblo, and 24 worked the commons. The latter had claims which, in due course, matured into ownership. This left 40 to be entered as landless. Of these, 25 are said to work for others on their land, and the remaining 15 simply existed."

By the time California had become a province of the Republic of Mexico in 1822, the climate, politically and commercially, had changed, and the southern portion had become more prominent than the northern one. Historian Remi Nadeau wrote, "Southern California had become a pastoral paradise for a new aristocracy. Most of the menial work was done by Indians who were not part of the mission system. The original crude huts of the pioneer rancheros gave way to rambling adobes that permitted gracious and hospitable living."

Then the Yankees started arriving—first a trickle, subsequently a flood—as did people from other nations. The first American to arrive in Los Angeles was Joseph Chapman, a Boston carpenter who discovered California in a uniquely romantic and exciting manner. Chapman supposedly was shanghaied by pirates in the streets of Boston, was carried to the Pacific Coast, escaped, joined a French buccaneer about to raid California, and was captured by Don Antonio Lugo during an attack on a Santa Barbara rancho. Saved by the ranch owner's daughter, Chapman redeemed himself by building a boat for the San Gabriel Mission padres, and by helping to finish the church that was built in the city plaza. Afterwards, completely vindicated, Chapman rode to Santa Barbara and brought back a bride, the very lady who saved his life by smiling at him when he was first captured.

[16]

Among the *gringos*, as the Mexicans called the Americans who arrived in Los Angeles during those early formative years, were James Pattie, who brought the first smallpox vaccine to California; William Wolfskill, a Kentuckian who planted the first orange groves and eucalyptus trees in California; Abel Stearns, a Massachusetts Yankee who had become a naturalized Mexican citizen, a wealthy businessman, and an owner of many large ranches; William Workman and John Rowland, two other Americans who had become naturalized Mexican citizens; Jonathan Warner, George Rice, Benjamin D. Wilson, John Reed, D. W. Alexander, Dr. John Marsh, plus a score more.

When the stream of American immigrants became a raging torrent and a definite threat to California's entity, Gov. Pio Pico lashed out, warning his countrymen:

"They are cultivating farms, establishing vineyards, erecting mills, sawing up lumber, building workshops, and doing a thousand other things which seem natural to them, but which Californians neglect or despise. What then are we to do? Shall we remain supine while those daring strangers are overrunning our fertile plains, and are gradually out- numbering and displacing us? Shall these incursions go unchecked, until we shall become strangers in our own land?"

Governor Pico's solution, drastic though it sounded, was simply a means of assuring the continuity of the Californians in positions of wealth and power. He advocated seces- sion from Mexico and the joining of California with either England or France, two coun- tries powerful enough to give protection and aid. Pico's words, however, were lost in the softly caressing ocean breezes, and in 1846, the war between Mexico and the United States was under way.

JEDEDIAH STRONG SMITH, one of the greatest of the mountain men, and his party of fifteen trap- pers were the first Americans to reach California, arriving at the San Gabriel Mission from the Great Salt Lake in 1826. Smith was the first to cross the Sierra Nevada, the Colorado River, and the Mojave Desert, facing constant danger, thirst, and starvation all the way. In this painting, he and his men are being greeted by the padres and Indians of the mission. (Title)

Since Mexican resistance was weak and sporadic, Los Angeles fell to the Yankee invaders on two occasions, the first time briefly, and the second time permanently. On August 7, 1846, an American squadron of marines under Commodore Robert F. Stockton anchored in San Pedro bay while Col. John C. Fremont was approaching Los Angeles from San Diego. Stockton and Fremont joined forces. Amazingly, they met no opposition, as Governor Pico and Gen. Jose Castro had abandoned the city, and the Americans easily marched forward and occupied Los Angeles without a shot being fired.

After about two weeks, Stockton and Fremont left the city, leaving it in the hands of Capt. Archibald H. Gillespie and a contingent of fifty men. Stockton went south to San Diego, where he immediately set sail for Monterey, and Fremont set off overland for San Francisco.

Gillespie, a rather nervous individual, frightened that a conspiracy he couldn't handle was taking place, moved with his garrison to the protection of Fort Hill. Soon, the conspiracy became a reality, and Gillespie eventually was forced to surrender. Fortunately, Angeleno insurgents allowed him to leave with his men and their supply of arms. With colors flying, they marched to San Pedro, where Gillespie took refuge on an American merchant ship.

In January of 1847, Commodore Stockton and Gen. Stephen W. Kearny, from San Diego, rode to the rescue. On January 8, the Battle of San Gabriel River, also called the Battle of El Paso de Bartolo Viejo (after the name of the rancho where the fighting took place), ended the war. Thus Los Angeles fell to the Americans for the second and last time. Instead of negotiating with Stockton and Kearny, however, the Californian forces, hoping for softer terms, chose to deal with Colonel Fremont, who had arrived at the San Fernando Mission on the day after the Americans marched into Los Angeles. A document signed on January 13, 1847, called the Treaty of Cahuenga, ended California's efforts to retain its own identity.

Los Angeles was incorporated as an American city on April 4, 1850, five months before California joined the Union. But it was not Los Angeles' independence that finally threw open Southern California to the world. It took the discovery of gold in California.

Until that time, Los Angeles had been virtually isolated, content to go its own way, with the rich getting richer and the poor getting poorer, as the saying goes. Life suddenly changed for the Angelenos, however, when gold was discovered up North at Sutter's Mill. Then the drizzle of humanity to the city became a deluge, and the old rancho life was gone forever.

The gold seekers streamed into the city from everywhere, but in particular from Sonora in Mexico and from the Southern states. Los Angeles was their stopping point, a midway station to the gold fields. They came over the southern part of the continent and buried the Los Angeles of the dons in a flurry of activity completely strange and incomprehensible to the elderly, fun-loving, placid Californians.

Money, which always had been scarce, now became plentiful. A cattle trade developed overnight. Cattle owners who were getting $2 a head for their beef, found themselves with offers of $50 a head, and in some cases prices zoomed higher. Everyone in the 1850s, it seemed, was walking around with money jingling in his pockets.

[18]

The prosperity would soon become tainted, though, and would develop into what some historians called the "cesspool of the nation." In the first year of the gold rush, the city's population took a drastic cut, from 5,000 to 1,600, but then the trend reversed itself when the fortune seekers came back from the gold country and changed Los Angeles as no others ever had before. They were thieves, bandits, murderers, and cutthroats, all of them seeking a hideout and a place of refuge. They were tired and disappointed prospectors, and they all intermingled to give Los Angeles its unsavory reputation. Throughout the vast Southwest, the inhabitants were referred to as *Los Diablos*, the Devils, and with justification.

Although many people poured in, this time from the north, Los Angeles remained a small city, contrary to expectations. Its business district had only one hotel. There were only a dozen stores, but many saloons and gambling places. There was a church, a jail, and one of the worst brothel districts ever put together anywhere.

It was a rough town, with much crime and violence, and, with an absence of law and order, arguments resulted in bloodletting on the spot. Mexicans utilized the knife in close combat, and the Americans used the gun, killing and wounding with bullets. Los Angeles in 1853 reported one death a day from fights and assassinations. Law enforcement was practically non-existent because sheriffs and marshals equally were victims.

If all this were not enough, Los Angeles with less than five thousand residents, suffered a drought in the early 1860s, and its effect was to finish off finally the dons and their big ranchos. Suddenly, people needed money. The stampede began, and herds of cattle were offered cheaply to anyone who had cash. But there were no buyers. Prices dropped quickly, then plunged to nothing. Cattle, dead or dying, were everywhere, and coyotes and

THE FIRST CITY HALL of Los Angeles under American rule was located on the front of a lot on the northwest corner of Spring and Jail, which afterward became Franklin Street. In the center of the lot, behind City Hall, was a baked-brick structure that was used as a jail. A new City Hall, however, was established in 1850, and was located directly opposite, where today stands Los Angeles' modern one at 200 North Spring Street. The 1850 City Hall was a long, one-story, adobe building which served for thirty years as a council chamber, a treasurer's office, a tax collector's office, and a residence for the city's jailer. (SPNB)

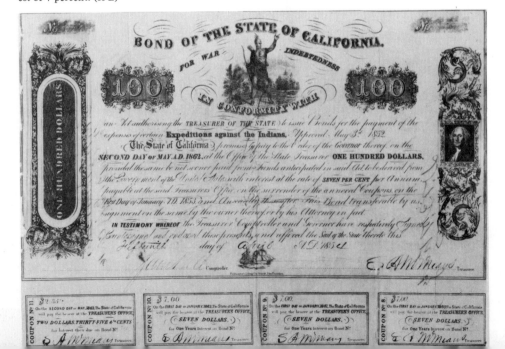

SKETCH of the BATTLE
OF
LOS ANGELE
UPPER CALIFORNIA
Fought
between the Americans
and Mexicans
JANY 9TH 1847.

THE LAST BATTLE in the war between the Californians (Mexicans) and the Yankees (Americans), for the pueblo of Los Angeles, took place on January 9, 1847, about four miles southeast of the pueblo's plaza, at what is now 4500 South Downey Road in the city of Vernon. The battle, known as the Battle of the Laguna or the Battle of the Mesa, was practically bloodless, and consisted of a half-hearted, unsuccessful cavalry charge by the Californian forces under the command of Jose Maria Flores. The next day, Yankee forces led by Commodore R. F. Stockton and Gen. Stephen W. Kearny marched into the pueblo and took it over. (SPNB)

[20]

DEFENSE BONDS are an old story in California history, as this 1852 note proves. Money raised from the sale of these bonds was used to pay off expenses incurred by the state in its expeditions against hostile Indians. The coupons on the bottom of the bond disclose that the obligations carried an interest of 7 percent. (H-E)

buzzards had a field day. There was hunger everywhere. The disaster was complete. Ranch owners, whose wealth was in cattle, went broke. They couldn't pay their taxes or their loans; financially crippled, they lost their great lands.

Without the cattle trade to support it, Los Angeles became a dead city. There were, however, individuals with foresight and vision. They came in 1868 and 1869 from Northern California and subdivided the land. Once more there was a flood of immigration, and by 1870 the city was again flourishing.

Thus Los Angeles went into the 1870s with a happy outlook. Its character was different, fortunately for the better. Growth was rapid, handsome houses were erected, new frame and brick structures replaced the adobes; and fire houses, shops, hotels, schools, banks, and factories suddenly blossomed into existence, altering the frontier look forever. Fields and orchards ran every which way, and whole communities, serving as market centers for farmers, grew up practically overnight.

Los Angeles was just pausing briefly to catch its breath when the financial panic sweeping the nation hit and ended all progress. Banks failed, and residents ran from the city in droves. By 1880, from a high of 16,000 persons, Los Angeles had shrunk to 11,000. But farm and real estate booms had been simmering since 1858, the year when the Butterfield stage line linked the area to the east, and it all of a sudden began to grow. The completion of the first transcontinental rail system to San Francisco in 1869 fanned the fire, and the coming of the Southern Pacific railroad to Los Angeles in 1876, and the Atchison, Topeka and Santa Fe in 1885 stoked the blaze. Not only did railroad competition spur new migration, since a price war permitted passengers to ride from the Missouri River to Los Angeles for $1, but it finally opened up Southern California to the rest of the nation. New types of people, farmers and businessmen, were arriving by the trainload to fuel the new prosperity, and it was the "Iron Horse" that made it possible.

LIFE IN LOS ANGELES in 1854 centered around the Plaza Church, today on a site where Sunset Boulevard meets Main Street. The town houses of the rancheros were located prominently in choice positions around the Plaza, while other homes were built on streets leading away. A common meeting place, the Plaza was where animals could graze, where young people could walk, and where children could play. (Title)

DON ANTONIO CORONEL, his wife, and servants were enjoying a musical moment at their home on Seventh and Alameda streets. Coronel, who arrived in Los Angeles in 1834 with his father, Don Ygnacio Coronel, was a scout with the Californian forces during the Mexican-American War. In 1850, he became the first assessory of Los Angeles County (encompassing what is now San Bernardino, Riverside, Imperial, Orange, and a large part of Kern County), and was mayor of Los Angeles in 1853. Also, Coronel helped start the Historical Society of Southern California, serving as one of its vice presidents in 1883. He died at age seventy-seven on April 17, 1894. (Title)

GEN. ANDREAS PICO, the brother of former Gov. Pio Pico, was the last Mexican military commander under Mexican rule in California, and signed the Treaty of Cahuenga for the Californians, ending the Mexican-American War in 1847. After the war, General Pico became an outstanding American citizen, and in 1859 led a fight to get the southern half of the state to secede and form a "Territory of Colorado," which was to be made up of cities from San Luis Obispo south. At one time Pico owned the 48,806-acre Los Coyotes ranch, north of Alamitos and east of Cerritos, and the 6,698 La Habra ranch. In addition, he owned a half-interest in the San Fernando Valley, which he had bought cheaply from Eulogio F. de Celis for only $15,000. Pico lived for a time on property he owned at the San Fernando Mission, and afterward moved into Los Angeles, where he died in 1876. (Alcana)

[22]

The great boom of the 1880s was under way. By the middle of 1886, the demand for land far exceeded the supply. There was a flood of hysterical buyers, and they pushed prices up by four hundred and five hundred percent in one year. Any lot could be sold anywhere at the drop of a surveyor's stake. New towns with strange-sounding names were laid out. Subdivisions were backed with big advertising and promotional campaigns. Prospective buyers were entertained with colorful parades and marching bands, and elephants and other circus animals were often trotted out. Auction sales, barbecues, and free tally-ho rides were offered as inducements. New lots, and even old ones, changed hands so often that there was barely enough time to make sales; if not in real estate offices, then in bars, in store corners, on the curb, in the street, or anywhere buyers and agents could get together. Promises, which were never intended to be kept, became hyperextravagant.

In 1887, during the height of the boom, more than sixty new towns were started. Twenty-five were on the Santa Fe route, and eight on the Southern Pacific. The others weren't on anything, and, in many cases, not even on maps!

A year later, the bubble burst. It started with the banks, which suddenly grew suspicious of the whole boom and began to hold back funds for the construction of new additions to subdivisions. When promoters, depending on financing in addition to the sale proceeds of previous developments, couldn't get money, it was virtually all over. As the money sources dried up, the entire structure collapsed.

By 1888, prices of real estate sagged, tumbled, and then hit rock bottom. Most promoters went broke, and towns became grain fields, many ghost towns. Even hotels, standing lonely and scattered throughout the boom areas—some only skeletons in the middle of nowhere—were left stranded and unfinished, places only for scavengers.

Yet, the real estate frenzy wasn't a complete disaster for Angelenos. Some good came out of it. What remained for them was a city of large, stately buildings, paved streets, new colleges, churches and schools, electric railroads, and street lights.

More importantly, everyone in the nation had heard of Los Angeles by 1890. The tide of people flowing to it may have slackened, but it was still the Promised Land.

A FAVORITE but brutal betting sport of the early 1850s and later was the *correr el gallo*. The roosters, their necks well greased, would be partially buried in the earth alongside a public road, with only their throat and head showing. Then riders on fast horses would dash by at full speed and try to grab the roosters and pull them out.
(Title)

[23]

FOR THOSE who couldn't leave town to chop wood, this type of wagon was a familiar and welcome sight during Los Angeles' formative years. Although these mules don't look too happy on the job, it was an important one, inasmuch as Angelenos had to wait until the late 1880s for gas, and until the early 1900s for electricity. Early vendors like this one did a booming business selling wood from door to door for use in cooking, lighting, and heating. (Title)

TO GET WATER to homes in early Los Angeles, wagons and animals had to cart it house to house from wells and rivers. As a result, the operation, in use even as late as 1854, was very expensive. Residents near the river or the Zanja Madre, an open ditch, in those days simply helped themselves, while others paid for the service. In one primitive form of delivery, local businessmen utilized donkeys and water bags, and charged about fifty cents a week for a bucket a day, excluding Sundays. (SPNB)

JOHN G. DOWNEY was the first Southern Californian to become governor during a time when few leading state officials were drawn from the Southland. Actually, Downey wasn't elected governor. Instead, he was elected lieutenant governor, and when Gov. Milton S. Latham became a United States senator, Downey finished out Latham's term. His political life was ruined, however, when it was suddenly revealed that he favored the Secessionists, and that he had advocated a bill for the apprenticing of Indians. Yet, when Downey returned to Los Angeles in 1860 with his wife, he was given a hero's welcome, with committee visits, receptions, speeches, and a thirteen-gun salute. Later, Downey helped relieve the 1868 water drought when he dug the area's first artesian well near present-day Compton, successfully tapping the underground basin for irrigation. That same year he opened the city's first bank, Hayward and Company, with John A. Hayward of San Francisco, and with others founded in 1873 what later would turn into the city's Chamber of Commerce. (Fraggi)

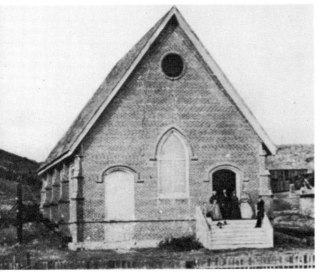

SAINT ATHANASIUS EPISCOPAL Church, the first Presbyterian house of worship in Los Angeles, was constructed in 1864 at Temple and New High streets, the approximate location of today's Los Angeles City Hall. The congregation worshipped in this imposing edifice until Christmas Day 1883 when Los Angeles County bought the site for a new Courthouse. (Title)

[25]

THIS RANCH, in what today is the Hollywood area, was the home of Jose Mascarel, who served as mayor of Los Angeles in 1865. Mascarel, in partnership with Juan Barri, a baker, owned a great deal of downtown Los Angeles property as well. He was a French sea captain who settled in Los Angeles in 1844, married an Indian, and became a successful merchant in Sonoratown at a time when the Mexican people in the community only traded with Latin-American storekeepers. (Title)

THIS HUGE WATER WHEEL was built in 1866 by Jean Louis Sainsevain under a Los Angeles city franchise, on the site of what is now North Broadway and the Los Angeles River. The wheel, which was imported in sections from San Francisco, lifted water in buckets from the river and sent it flowing through the open ditch, the Zanja Madre, to the city and outlying areas, where it was purchased by residents and farmers. The wheel was destroyed by a rain storm in 1868, and pipes were used thereafter. Years later the ditch was filled, parts of which are under today's Los Angeles Street. (LADWP)

[26]

THE TALLEST BUILDING in Los Angeles in 1868 was probably the Los Angeles County Courthouse, which boasted a spire above a huge steeple clock that, because of its four faces, could be seen for miles around. Located in the entire block between Main, Court, Market, and Spring streets, the two-story Courthouse of brick painted brown had four or five steps leading to its sidewalk on the Main Street side. It served until 1890, when a new Courthouse was constructed. (Title)

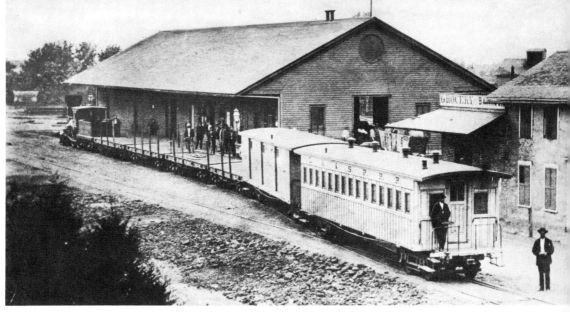

THE FIRST RAILROAD, built by the issuance of $150,000 in Los Angeles County bonds and $75,000 in Los Angeles city bonds, stretched twenty-two miles long to Wilmington. Starting operations in October 1869, its freight house, at the corner of Commercial and Alameda streets, also served as the passenger depot and contained the company's general offices. Freight rates were $5 per ton on groceries, $6 per ton on dry goods. Passengers paid $1.50 each to Wilmington.

IN 1870, THE PLAZA CHURCH, with its gazebo bell tower, looked about as it did when construction ended in 1822, and still stands at its original location. To get the church started in 1818, citizens contributed five hundred head of cattle, which were taken by the governor, who had promised to include funds for construction in his next year's budget. When he reneged on his promise, construction halted. San Gabriel Mission padres then contributed seven barrels of brandy worth $575, and construction continued. However, in 1821 work stopped again, but was resumed after other missions contributed more brandy, and parishioners donated wine, more cattle, and mules.

ALTHOUGH the San Fernando Mission conducted a private school around 1840, the first public school for the San Fernando Valley was established in 1869 under the direction of Mr. and Mrs. Geronimo Lopez, and was located at Lopez Station, an adobe built as a stage house and stable but never used as such. About three miles from the mission, the school, taught in English, was partly free and partly by subscription. It had twenty-five students, and paid its teacher, Mrs. Catherine Carter, $60 a month. (Title)

[27]

IN AN ATTEMPT to recapture the glory and charm of the California era under Mexican rule, former Gov. Pio Pico built the Pico House facing the Plaza on the site of the Jose Antonio Carrillo home. The hotel was completed in 1869, and for a decade truly was the finest in Southern California. It was used for balls, weddings, receptions, and honeymoons, and was host to every distinguished guest in the city. All of its rooms were gas-lit, and it boasted of baths on its second and third floors. Pico spent $50,000 for the building and afterwards poured in another $35,000 to furnish the hotel's eighty-plus rooms. (Alcana)

[28]

ONE OF THE PIONEER Los Angeles families was that of Dennis Sullivan, who homesteaded a portion of Los Angeles now bounded by Vermont, Melrose, and Normandie avenues, and Santa Monica Boulevard. Sullivan, who had had only a few Mexican ranchers as neighbors when plowing his fields in the early 1870s, lived to see his property absorbed by Los Angeles as it grew quickly from a pueblo to a major city by the early 1900s. The property totaled 160 acres, part of which today is the site of Los Angeles City College. (Title)

ON THE SECOND FLOOR of this Downey Block building above the L. W. Thatcher sign, an organization which was the forerunner of the Los Angeles Public Library, opened its doors after it was organized at a meeting in the Merced Theater on December 7, 1872. Called the Los Angeles Library Association, members paid $50 for a lifetime card and $5 for annual privelages, and named J. C. Littlefield as its first librarian. When the organization was taken over by the City of Los Angeles in 1889, it was the beginning of the Los Angeles Library system. Its collection of 6000 volumes was removed from the Downey Block headquarters to rooms in a new City Hall on Broadway.

[29]

LOS ANGELES' FIRST HIGH SCHOOL was located where First Street and Hill is now, and was built in 1873 at a cost of $20,000. Standing above the city and overlooking the old Courthouse on the right, it had Dr. W. T. Lucky, superintendent of schools, as its first principal. Its first class was graduated in 1875 with seven students. In 1882 it was removed to California Street (now Fort Moore Hill, where the present Los Angeles Board of Education building stands) to make room for a Los Angeles County Courthouse. (Title)

THE SOUTHERN DISTRICT AGRICULTURAL SOCIETY opened its first fair at Agricultural Park in 1871. Although subsidized by the state for the promotion of agriculture, the park's principal and most absorbing feature was its racetrack. Quasi-publically owned, it offered gambling concessions, Sunday rabbit hunts, and other entertainment. Around the turn of the century, when members of the Sixth Agricultural District started selling off its land and subdividing the property, a fight started by citizens of Los Angeles to save the park. In 1911, Exposition Park, which still exists, was the result, opening on 114 acres of Agricultural Park property where today stands the Los Angeles Memorial Coliseum and the Los Angeles Sports Arena. (SPNB)

THE FIRST JEWISH SYNAGOGUE, Congregation B'nai B'rith, was built in 1872, a striking brick structure located on the east side of Fort Street (now Broadway) between Second and Third streets. It was the forerunner to the Wilshire Boulevard Temple, dedicated in 1929. Prior to the building of its own temple, Los Angeles' Jewish congregation held services in the 1860s at Stearns Hall, and afterwards in Leck's Hall, a two-story building on Main Street between Second and Third streets. The ground floor of the hall was a grocery kept by Lorenzo Leck, and the meeting place, above the grocery, was a large, bare apartment. (Title)

CHARLES E. MILES was the first famous volunteer fire foreman (chief) because of his flashy white-shirted uniform and the chief's emblem on his shirtfront. In 1874, he ran Engine Company No. 1 on Spring Street, and during his leadership used the city's first hook and ladder, which was built by a local firm. Since the equipment proved too heavy and awkward, however, it later was sold to Wilmington. In 1876, Miles was elected chief of the city's first organized volunteer fire department, and served for one year. (LAFD)

[30]

UNTIL THE RAILROADS came to Los Angeles, the burden of growth for the area fell on its various stage lines, which carried both freight and passengers. For example, from 1874 to 1876, while the first transcontinental railroad was being built toward the city, train passengers rode to the end of the track and traveled the rest of the way in stagecoaches. Such a station was maintained at Mojave by Wells Fargo and Company for this purpose.

OWNERS of this Los Angeles and Independence Railroad in 1875 had visions of connecting the West Coast with Independence, Missouri. Instead, the line ran from Los Angeles to Santa Monica, via Beverly Hills. The Los Angeles end of the line was this depot, which opened to traffic in 1875 at Sixth and San Pedro streets. Note the depot's fancy Victorian style of architecture. (H-E)

THE FAMOUS QUEEN ANNE GUEST COTTAGE owned by Elias Jackson "Lucky" Baldwin stands restored today at the Los Angeles State and County Arboretum on what used to be Baldwin's Santa Anita rancho. The ranch, a sprawling 80,000 acres, from 1875 until after the turn of the century, stretched across the San Gabriel Valley from the Sierra Madre to the Puente Hills, and was a broad expanse of orchards, vineyards, and pastures. Baldwin, who parlayed mining stocks into one of America's great fortunes, turned the woods surrounding his home into a deer park, imported peacocks from India and Java, and built a training track for his thoroughbred horses, many of them stake winners. Baldwin purchased the ranch for $200,000 from Harris Newmark and Company. (Title)

[32]

ALTHOUGH LOS ANGELES was growing as a city in 1876, it was still considered a raw town, as evidenced by the man with a rifle in foreground and the team of oxen at right. That year, however, Los Angeles saw the completion of the Southern Pacific line between the city and San Francisco, with a celebration at Soledad above the tunnel and a banquet for 400 residents of both cities in Los Angeles' Union Hall. It was also the year that the city purchased its first hook-and-ladder truck, which was hauled to fires by hand.

THE JACOBY BROS. in 1879 was probably the city's most successful clothing and dry goods establishment. Subsequently, as business boomed, Jacoby Bros., led by Nathan Jacoby, expanded into its own building, which was still standing in the downtown area when Nathan died in 1911. When the store's staff posed in front of its Main Street location, Los Angeles had a population of 45,000, and city property was assessed at $18 million. That same year saw the start of the new City Hall on Fort Street, and the public school system boasted of 5,302 children in its classes, and of 100 teachers who were paid an average of $85 per month. (Title)

THE FIRST BAND at the University of Southern California in the early 1880s included coeds who sang along with the group. Some of the musicians wore whiskers but, unlike today, did not take the risk of catching long hair in their instruments. The band rode to the campus on horseback or by buggy, and practiced by kerosene light. Keeping a close watch on the band was Dr. Marion M. Bovard (extreme left), who was the first university president, serving from 1880 to 1891. (USC)

ONE OF THE HIGHEST PRICES paid for a home was recorded in 1880 when I. N. Van Nuys purchased from M. J. Newmark his residence next to the corner of Spring and Seventh streets. The transaction was for $6,500, which was $1,000 less than what it had cost to build the home. Also, Van Nuys paid $425 for the adjoining corner lot, which around the 1930s became the site of the Van Nuys Building, occupied in part by the Los Angeles First National Bank. (SPNB)

[33]

THREE HORSES PULLED this pump through the Los Angeles streets in 1880, approximately six years before the city established a salaried fire department. Until 1886, the department was an all-volunteer outfit, with the various companies going in different directions. In the driver's seat in this picture is Walter S. Moore, the city's first chief engineer. Riding on the back of the pump is fireman Frank Angelke. (LAFD)

THE TELEPHONE, introduced in 1882, started with seven subscribers, the first being at the Southern Pacific Railroad River Station. Soon after, these operators were hired. By 1886, Los Angeles had 1,050 telephones, with 200 others set up in county towns. The girls on duty were famous for their long and flowing skirts, and for being required to stand while working.

MIRROR PRINTING, BINDING AND RULING was an establishment in 1872 that occupied the upper portion of this annex of the Downey Block, with a separate entrance off Temple Street. About ten years later, in 1882, when this picture was taken, Col. Harrison Gray Otis, with Yarnell, Caystile, and Mathes, purchased both [34] Mirror Printing and the *Times* newspaper. In 1883, the *Times-Mirror* was issued as a weekly, and the Times-Mirror Company was incorporated with capital stock worth some $40,000. (Title)

THIS STORE in 1882 served the people who lived around Aliso Street east of Beverly Boulevard, in what today is East Los Angeles. The area was named by Dr. J. S. Griffin, who received 2,000 acres east of the Los Angeles River from the city for services performed during a smallpox epidemic in 1863. Ten years later, Griffin subdivided his land, called it East Los Angeles, and sold off lots. (Title)

THE CAHUENGA VALLEY TOWNSHIP SCHOOL in 1884, although serving an area sparsely populated, had an unusually large group of students, all of whom, it seems, turned out for this picture. When pictures were taken in those days, even the animals were brought in. The horse was used by the youth for transportation to and from the school. (Title)

THIS LIQUOR AND CIGAR STORE did a booming business on the southwest corner of Main and Third streets in 1884. It was constructed in the late 1870s, and was torn down about thirty years later to make room for a Citizens National Bank building. (Title)

[36] MEMBERS OF THE FIRST TENNIS CLUB in Southern California posed proudly for a photographer on July 12, 1884. The club was formed by the men and women of the city of San Gabriel, and met at the "old" Purcell home on the Las Tunas Ranch in San Gabriel County. The five children sitting on the ground to the left were (left to right) Geoffrey M. Purcell, Helen A. Purcell, Launcelot M. Purcell, Norah Purcell, and Hugh G. Purcell. Three years later the Southern California Tennis Association was founded in Riverside at the "Whitehouse." (Title)

THE CORNER of New High and Republic streets in Sonoratown in 1885 featured a saloon that was a gathering place on a quiet morning for residents. Republic was a short street, no more than one hundred feet long, below the Plaza Church. From the corner of New High and Republic, Prudent Beaudry, who had his offices in a two-story building, could look down the length of the street and across Main, and see the Pico House. (Title)

A SUMMER RESORT around the Arroyo Seco (dry riverbed) in the Pasadena area was operated in 1885 by a jeweler, C. P. Switzer. Supplies and guests were brought into the camp by donkey, and were protected by rifle-toting guards, who also rode donkeys. The Arroyo Seco was a quiet place that gave guests an opportunity to catch up on their reading (note the tent and the women with books in front). (Title)

HISTORIC HALE HOUSE, built in the mid-1880s at 4425 North Figueroa Street in Highland Park, was a stylish home of a Queen Anne-Eastlake type of architecture. Apparently scorning architects, the carpenters of the day yielded to the Victorian influence and crammed everything under one gabled roof, with a liberal application of carved wood inside and out. Also unusual about the house was its coloring. The first floor was in several shades of an earthy turquoise and the second floor and attic were an earthy red. Smaller details were in a brownish yellow. Today, the home stands restored in Los Angeles Heritage Square, and is listed in the National Register of Historic Places. (CHB)

"TOWNBALL," now known as baseball, was the name given to the sport this team played in the 1880s in Los Angeles. In those early days teams competed whenever and wherever they could, picking up unscheduled games much the way our sandlot teams do today. Note the uniforms and the various individualistic neck pieces. Also, note the old catcher's mask. This team just looks like a winning combination! (Title)

LOS ANGELES in 1885, looking east over the city toward Sixth and Hill streets with St. Vincent's College on the right: It was the year that Los Angeles public schools introduced music to their curricula; Dr. Sketchley, a naturalist, established his Ostrich Farm near where Glendale is today; the first medical school, a branch of USC, was founded; and the old *zanza* water system was finally abandoned. (Title)

THE MAIN STREET RAILWAY COMPANY became a reality in 1875 when its tracks extended from Temple Block to Washington streets. Afterwards, it was run along Jefferson Street and Wesley Avenue to the racetrack at Agricultural Park, where its barn was located. Still later, a branch was built out Washington to Figueroa Avenue, and down Figueroa back to Jefferson. The railway company was still going strong in 1886, when these tracks were laid at Main Street and Third. However, in 1897, as the last horse-car disappeared from Los Angeles streets, the line, which had held out the longest against progress, finally became part of the city's electrical transportation system. (Title)

[39]

SOME OF THE LARGEST PUMPKINS ever seen in California were grown on this farm in the San Fernando Valley in 1886. In later years, after water was brought down to Los Angeles from the Owens Valley, the San Fernando Valley was transformed overnight from a grain-raising community dependent on intermittent rainfall to an empire of truck gardens and orchards, and became one of the richest agricultural communities in the world. (SPNB)

LOS ANGELES, after it was founded in 1781 near the old Plaza on the bank of the Los Angeles River, soon evolved into Sonoratown, a Mexican community. By 1887, the town had changed little, despite this picture of brick buildings and white-washed fronts of homes. Until the late 1870s it was an unsavory place where Americans went to drink, smoke, dance, and gamble. It was a place where the adobe home flourished, from great rectangle buildings with patios in the center to one- or two-room huts. A visit to Sonoratown was like stepping from an American town into a small Mexican pueblo which still retained its language, dress, customs, and traditions, despite the closeness of the new homes, businesses, and influence of its English-speaking neighbors. (Title)

THE PICO STREET and Maple Avenue Electric Railway, the first electric railway in the world, was a crudely operated trolley train that was born in 1887 and died the same year for lack of patronage. It ran from the Plaza through downtown along Maple to Pico Street, and west on Pico to Lerdo, now Harvard Boulevard. It was specifically operated to take people to the Electric Homestead Tract, a development along West Pico. The lots sold slowly, however, and the railway passed into oblivion, lacking sufficient capital to continue operation. (SPNB)

ONE OF THE CITY'S MAIN THOROUGHFARES, Spring Street, with its Baker Block (far right), saw business conducted as usual after the boom years of 1885 and 1886. During 1887, when this picture was taken facing north from First Street, Spring was paved. The Los Angeles Theater was constructed between Second and Third streets, and a large, frame building, which had served so long as a public gathering place, was sold by the Turnverein Germania, a German club, to L. J. Rose and J. B. Lankershim. After it was removed to another lot, a brick hall costing $40,000 was erected on the site.

[41]

WHEAT GROWING and harvesting was a major industry, as this picture indicates, in the San Fernando Valley in 1887. One vast wheat field, the valley's ranches combined to produce more than 500,000 bushels. A typical harvesting scene, the work was under way on the Van Nuys Ranch, located north of the Rancho Encino. (Title)

WILLIAM HAYES PERRY, one of Los Angeles' oldest pioneers, built this regal residence at Brooklyn Avenue near Sixth Street in Boyle Heights around 1887. Perry spared no expense in making his home one of the most beautiful, refined, and best in Los Angeles, and surrounded it with trees, gardens, a greenhouse, a guest house, and a panoramic view of the city. When Perry arrived in Los Angeles in 1853, he was a penniless carpenter. When he died in 1906, he was reportedly one of Los Angeles' wealthiest individuals. (Title)

CENTRAL ELEMENTARY SCHOOL was moved in this fashion from Poundcake Hill to Sand Street, a few blocks away, in 1887. The wooden structure reverted to being an elementary school when Los Angeles High School moved off the hill in 1885 to another location. How the building was moved seems mystifying, even today, but it did force the contractor, whose costs became more than he expected, into bankruptcy. (Title)

ALTHOUGH THERE WERE NO PAVED ROADS or sidewalks for bicycle riders in 1887, there were still plenty of wide-open spaces through which the riders could easily pedal. Here is a picture of the Los Angeles Bicycle Club when members stopped for a rest in a desolate stretch of land outside of Los Angeles. Most of the men were wearing their "Sunday" best, and some wouldn't be seen dead without their hats. (Title)

HOTEL ARCADIA, completed in the Santa Monica area in 1887, was probably the finest suburban hotel in Southern California. Named after Dona Arcadia, wife of Col. R. S. Baker, it was built four-stories high on a bluff overlooking the ocean, had a great verandah and side wings, and a center tower and cupola. Its proprietor was J. W. Scott. From the oceanside, hotel guests could see incoming and outgoing ships in the Santa Monica harbor. From the other side, guests could see parts of Los Angeles off in the distance. (Alcana)

LONG BEACH was a booming city in 1887 when this picture was taken looking north along Pine Avenue, with the First Street intersection in foreground. In July 1887, H. G. Wilshire (after whom Los Angeles' Wilshire Boulevard was named) offered lots at $150 and up for "Peerless Long Beach," and advertised the city as a prosperous town of 2,000 persons. Although this intersection, where the city's first house was built, was a busy one, not far from it sheep were still being herded on the bluff overlooking the ocean. (LB)

PASADENA'S RAYMOND HOTEL was completed in 1887, the year the Los Angeles and Pasadena Railway began carting passengers between the hotel and Los Angeles. The hotel, which catered exclusively to tourists and vacationers, was built on a knoll overlooking the surrounding towns and orange groves. This picture taken in 1887 shows the first train to stop at the Raymond Avenue Station and its load of hotel guests, who either had to ride by carriage or walk to the hotel. Note the Raymond Hotel in the background, sticking up behind the train. (Title)

ONE OF THE FIRST HOTELS to cater to tourists, the Belmont, caught fire and burned down in 1888, The hotel was a three-story structure with verandahs, located on a hill site improved with lawn and sand shrubbery at First and Belmont streets, near the end of the Second Street cable railroad. (Title)

AS THE CITY BRANCHED OUT in different directions in the 1880s, Main Street took on a new look. The bulk of the city's retail business was still accomplished between the Plaza and the Temple Block, but further south the street became a high-class residential neighborhood, as this picture shows north of Fifth Street in 1888. (Title)

THE SAN FERNANDO MISSION, which was secularized by the Mexicans and ceded back to the Catholic Church in 1862 by a decree of Pres. Abraham Lincoln, was disintegrating by 1888 from years of disuse. In this picture that year, a group of local residents study the crumbling church. Afterward, sporadic attempts were made to preserve and repair it. The most ambitious efforts were undertaken by the Landmarks Club in 1897, when a temporary roof was installed, and in 1916, when the roof again was replaced. In 1938, a final restoration program was started by "Friends of Mission San Fernando," and the work was completed in 1950. It was the seventeenth mission, and founded September 8, 1797. (Title)

THE HONEYMOON ELEVATOR, on the Los Angeles County Courthouse building (the only outdoor passenger elevator in the United States when it was constructed around 1888) gave the city a "loving" reputation throughout the world. The elevator was famous for carrying couples to the marriage license bureau on the third floor of the courthouse. After about forty years of service to the love-life of the city, the elevator became too dangerous to use and was condemned by county supervisors. (H-E)

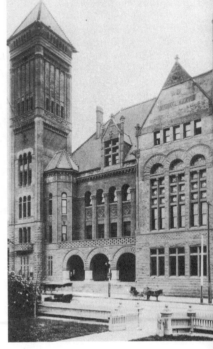

LOS ANGELES' SECOND CITY HALL, completed in 1889 on Broadway between Second and Third streets, was an elaborate building which gained attention throughout the Southland for being an architectural showcase. It was used for about forty years, and then sold at auction piece by piece after a more modern structure, which still stands today at Spring and First streets, was opened in 1928. When the Broadway City Hall was built, the street was still a semi-residential avenue, with homes, lawns, and flowers in evidence. Note that horse-drawn wagons and carriages were still the main forms of transportation.

THE FIRST SCHOOL in the town of Lankershim in 1889 was conducted in a bunk house on the Lankershim Ranch. Before the area became part of Los Angeles, it was sold by the Lankershim Ranch, Land and Water Company in lots of varying sizes, chiefly 40-acre parcels for $5 to $150 an acre. First the parcels were banded together as Toluca, then as Lankershim, and finally after being annexed to Los Angeles in 1927, the area became officially known as North Hollywood. (SPNB)

TODAY'S SECURITY PACIFIC NATIONAL BANK started business in 1889 as the Security Savings Bank and Trust Company in the Weil Building at 148 South Main Street. Located below the Los Angeles Business College, the bank had $200,000 in capital, and had George H. Bonebrake as president. (SPNB)

LOS ANGELES' DOUBLE-TRACK CABLE RAILWAY opened with a bang in 1889, and few years later went out with a whimper. This picture on August 3, 1889, shows the ceremonies which were conducted on the First Street bridge to mark the opening of a section of it to Boyle Heights. Speeches were held, and fireworks were set off in the evening. Approximately $1 million was invested in track and equipment, but in a few years, due to excessive operating expenses and lagging public support, it finally failed and was succeeded by another system.

ALTHOUGH BROADWAY was a busy street in 1889, it did little for the city's new and experimental cable-car system. The cables suffered excessive wear, and the machinery often broke down. In time of heavy rains and floods, the conduits filled with sand and gravel and halted operations until repairs could be made. Broadway saw other changes, too, that year, when Fort Street south of First was changed to Broadway. However, it wasn't until 1910 that the rest of the street north of First also became Broadway, losing historic Buena Vista and Downey streets forever from city maps.

THE ICE CREAM MAN, Nicolas Martinez, was probably the first of the many oddball people who have been attracted to Los Angeles over the years since its founding. Martinez, who was of Mexican-Indian birth and about forty years old, always wore a white canvas suit and carried a huge bucket on his head. He walked the main Los Angeles streets, including those of Sonoratown, every night from about 7 p.m. to midnight. In the fall and winter, Martinez sold tamales, but switched to ice cream in the summer. Here he's pictured in 1890, at the height of his popularity, with his ice cream bucket on his head. (Title)

Forging Ahead:
1890 to 1899

AS SOON AS THE REAL ESTATE BUBBLE burst, Los Angeles settled down to a new life and changed without warning from an old city to a very young one. Its population in 1890 hit 50,000, three-fourths of which were virtual newcomers. These new people, who shoved aside those who had settled earlier, bluntly and aggressively arranged the land to suit themselves, just as the Spaniards had done in the beginning to the Indians, and as the Americans had done afterward to the Californians.

Then Edward L. Doheny and his partner stirred things up. They dug a hole in the city's downtown residential district and came up with "black gold." If Doheny could hit oil, others were sure they could too, and didn't even bother to clear off their lots. They rushed to put up derricks on front lawns, in back yards, and through the floors of living rooms and bedrooms. Some became rich, and they changed Los Angeles forever. Soon after, the nation's financial panic caught up with the West Coast and closed four banks. City fathers, however, wouldn't sit still, and they came up with a solution. In an attempt to end the depression and to alleviate the area's economic ills, they decided the least they could do was have a party. Out of this philosophy came the enormously successful La Fiesta celebrations. Suddenly, everything was actually better.

The horse-car disappeared from city streets, and transportation began running on electricity. Henry Huntington, realizing there was a fortune to be made in the pueblo, came from San Francisco and, without any fanfare, began to buy up railroad properties. At the same time that Henry was beginning his transportation empire, there was a fight over a location for the city's harbor site. One faction favored Santa Monica; the other pushed San Pedro. When the smoke cleared in Washington, D. C., where the decision was made, the winner was San Pedro.

Best of all the happenings in this period was that Los Angeles did not have to pay a cent for 3,000 acres of land right in the heart of the city. They were a gift from Col. Griffith J. Griffith, and they became Griffith Park, one of the largest parks in the world.

THE FIRE DEPARTMENT would have been severely handicapped without the use of horses around the 1890s, inasmuch as some of its steamers and hook-and-ladder trucks in service at the time weighed well over four tons. The hills of First Street also posed a problem, and many times in rushing to a fire the men had to jump off and help push.

THESE CHINESE SCHOOL CHILDREN in 1890 were the descendants of those Chinese who originally left China to join the Gold Rush. Afterwards, in 1869, about fifty Chinese came to Los Angeles and settled south of the Plaza. As others arrived, they settled alongside the original colony. By 1870, there were about two hundred Chinese living in Los Angeles. The first Chinatown in Los Angeles included much of the old Plaza and the area surrounding it, especially along Alameda Street. Today, the city's large Chinese community is established approximately seven blocks north of City Hall. (Title)

AS THE CITY MOVED SOUTH, spreading out from the downtown area, businesses followed along. One of the more prominent establishments in 1890 was this Broad-Guage Department Store, and also Fisher's Hardware Store, both located on South Main Street north of Washington, near where the wealthier residents were building mansions. (Title)

A PICNIC to raise funds for a church bell at Swan's Valley on Catalina Island turned out almost all of the island's settlers around 1890. It was an enthusiastic group that was entertained by guitar and mandolin players, who are seated on the ground in the foreground. (Title)

MEXICAN CALIFORNIANS wait for a ride in front of the Convento building at the San Fernando Mission sometime in the 1880s or 1890s. During those days, the mission was deserted, and anyone could walk in and use its facilities, which were falling apart from lack of care. At one time the mission was used as a storehouse, and even as a stopping place for the Butterfield Stage. (Title)

A VIEW OF RANCHO EL ENCINO and of its vast fields in 1890 in the San Fernando Valley: The ranch, originally a Spanish land grant of 4,400 acres, was within the approximate boundaries of White Oak and Vanowen avenues and Sepulveda and Ventura boulevards, and had been acquired by Vicente de la Osa. Osa built and lived in an adobe house, which is still standing. The home afterward was used by Eugene Garnier, later by the Amestoy family, and now is a state historical monument. (Title)

[51]

THE WEDDINGTON BROTHERS general store, run by Guy and Fred, was the first business to open in North Hollywood in the late 1880s and the early 1890s on the old Lankershim Ranch, on what today is the North Hollywood business district. The store was located in the middle of an apricot grove in a sparsely settled area near the Southern Pacific depot. It served the south half of the San Fernando Valley, and drew customers from as far away as Calabassas, some thirty miles from the store. Not only was the store the community post office, but it was a political and speech-making center as well. (SPNB)

THE STEAM RAILROADS were in command until the arrival of the electric railroads on the Los Angeles scene. This steamer ran from the late 1880s to about 1895 when it was replaced by an electric. It ran from the northwest part of Los Angeles toward the Cahuenga Pass, along the foothills and the mesa by way of Colgrove Avenue and South Hollywood, to the ocean at Santa Monica, then called North Beach. (Title)

IN THE 1880s AND EARLY 1890s, when the Southern Pacific Railroad was at the height of its popularity, excursion trains ran passengers from Los Angeles to Santa Monica, where they would walk or ride to the beach and other tourist attractions. Later, the "Big Red Cars" would put the Southern Pacific out of business, but in the meantime, in the 1880s, the railroad helped the great land boom that had been built up by Easterners and Midwesterners who were arriving in Los Angeles by the thousands. (Title)

THE CORNES AND SLOSSON Livery Feed and Sale Stable was one of the more prosperous businesses in Monrovia at the time of this picture in 1892. Not only did it deal with Monrovian residents, but also with customers from the surrounding smaller towns and communities. Monrovia was founded six years earlier, when the area's first settler, William N. Monroe, after whom the city was named, started selling town lots from the 240 acres he owned. Values rose so quickly, that in less than a year the lots in the business district were selling for $100 per front foot. (Title)

WHEN BICYCLING became a popular local sport, following the roller skating fad of the 1870s and early 1880s, racing also became popular. Competitions were held on various courses, but mostly on a road between Los Angeles and Santa Monica, on a quarter-mile track at Seventh Street and Alameda, or at Agricultural Park. In 1885, the Los Angeles Wheelmen became a national league club, and cycling fever became rampant. Here is the Riverside Bicycling team in competition on October 2, 1893. (Title)

REDONDO BEACH in the late 1890s and the early 1900s discovered that its carnation fields were tourist attractions along with its busy pier, famous hotel, and Redondo Beach plunge. Billed as a seaside resort city in those days, the Pacific Electric Railway carried passengers on excursions from Los Angeles to the city, where the bulk of the visitors would flock to the hotel, which was then known for its tennis, bathing parties, luncheons, dinners, balls, and even dances for the younger set. (Title)

[53]

CHESTER PLACE, one of the most exclusive residential neighborhoods in Los Angeles, was developed as a subdivision by Judge Charles Silent, whose house is in this picture of the 1890s. The area, originally eighteen acres, was behind Saint Vincent's Church at the corner of Figueroa Street and West Adams Boulevard. Judge Silent, who had arrived in Los Angeles from San Jose, cultivated exotic, semi-tropical flowers, many of which remained with the magnolias, pines, and rubber trees on the property which originally had included twelve homes and was surrounded by wrought iron fences and huge gates. In later years, Mr. and Mrs. Edward Laurence Doheny, who were the first to hit oil in Los Angeles, bought as much of Chester Place as possible. Eventually, the Dohenys tore down Judge Silent's home in order to create more garden space. (Title)

[54]

PART OF THE "LONGSTREET TRACT," this two-story mansion at the corner of Adams Boulevard and Flower Street about 1893 belonged to Charles Longstreet, who sold it in the late 1890s to John Singleton after a fire destroyed much of the estate. Singleton restored the Southern-style mansion and added other buildings, including a magnificent stable. After 1900, a second fire destroyed all the buildings in "Singleton Court," as it was then called, with the exception of the stable and a garden tea house. John Brockman, a pioneer and wealthy businessman, subsequently purchased the property, but instead of rebuilding, turned it into Brockman Park, which became famous to Angelenos in the early 1900s. In 1921, Brockman donated the estate to the Los Angeles Orthopaedic Foundation, which already had established a clinic in 1917 in a house on South Figueroa Street. (Title)

JOHN H. BARTLE was a Monrovia real estate developer and banker who settled in the area in 1885. He was head of a group which started the First National Bank of Monrovia, and was a city trustee, chairman of the board of trustees, and a Monrovia city treasurer. The Bartle family took this picture on the steps of their two-story frame house, which also contained two stores and offices, on Myrtle Avenue in the 1890s. The home was destroyed by fire in 1897, and was rebuilt of brick. (Title)

THE LOS ANGELES CABLE RAILWAY to East Los Angeles had been operating for five years when this picture was taken in 1894. The end of the line in Los Angeles started at Jefferson Street, ran north on Grand Avenue to Seventh Street, went east to Broadway, north to First Street, east to Spring Street, north to the Plaza, then to San Fernando Street, over the Southern Pacific tracks, across the bridge over the river, and out Downey Avenue to Gates Street at the other end. (H-E)

ONE OF THE EARLIEST of the La Fiesta parades, an annual event for more than forty years, passed in review at its conclusion in Fiesta Park at the corner of Pico Boulevard and Grand Avenue. The first Fiesta, originated by Max Meyberg of the Los Angeles Merchants' Association, was held in 1894 in order to entice people from San Francisco to Los Angeles and stimulate a lagging economy. It was a joyous, Spanish-flavored event with a queen, a parade, brass bands, and colorfully designed horse-drawn carriages. (SPNB)

COLLEGE STUDENTS, even medical students, had their humorous side in 1894, just as college youths have today. Here's a wagon load of University of Southern California Medical College students participating in the city's first La Fiesta parade. On their way to the conclusion of the parade in Fiesta Park, they're moving on the west side of Main, between Seventh and Eighth streets. (Title)

THE LIST OF PATRONESSES for the first La Fiesta ball included almost all of the leading social names in the city. The ball was held on Friday evening of April 13, 1894, at Hazard's Pavilion, and climaxed four days of fun-filled activities which started April 10. Instead of being jinxed by being held on a Friday the 13th, on the contrary, the ball proved to be a delightful affair.

SOCIETY LEADERS, businessmen, and politicians, including Mayor Frank Rader, crammed into the stands in front of the old City Hall in 1895 to watch the second La Fiesta parade. As this picture was taken, the Americus Club, to the cheers of the crowd, marched past in review. This second La Fiesta was a more ostentatious display than the first, with more pomp and ceremony scheduled. In addition, gasoline torches were used to light up the night pageant, because the electrical lighting system was considered inadequate. (H-E)

QUEEN OF LOS ANGELES' second La Fiesta in 1895 was Mrs. C. Modini Wood, who was chosen from among the reigning society belles of her day. During the parade and celebration, she wore jewelry on her arm and gown in addition to her jeweled crown and richly embroidered regal robe.

THE GANG at the Los Angeles Gas Company found time to pose in 1895. Those identified were (1) S. E. Bangerter, (2) Addison B. Day, and (3) Charles A. Bartlett. The Gas Company was formed in 1865 by W. H. Perry, who after five years sold out at a huge profit. To get his franchise, Perry had to supply free gas for lights in the mayor's office and free gas for key Main Street crossings. By 1870, however, gas lighting still had a long way to go. On all of Los Angeles Street there was only one gas lamp! (Fraggi)

PASS SCHOOL STUDENTS in the mid-1890s took time out from studies to pose for a photographer. Located in the North Hollywood area of the Cahuenga Valley on Pass Road at about where Sunset Boulevard and Gordon Street is today, the school contained three classrooms which were overcrowded because of an influx of settlers to the valley. A new schoolhouse was later built at another location at the urging of the Cahuenga Valley Improvement Association. (Title)

JOHN BRADBURY, a young millionaire, and his wife, the former Lucy Banning, daughter of Gen. Phineas Banning, were a familiar sight to Los Angeles residents in the middle 1890s. Here they are pictured driving their fine horses from a flower-decorated carriage in one of the early Los Angeles La Fiesta parades. In later years, Mrs. Bradbury, renowned as the most beautiful belle in California, was divorced from Bradbury and figured in several ill-starred romances. She died in Italy in 1929. (H-E)

ANGELENOS DEARLY LOVED A PARADE, and La Fiesta of 1896 gave them an opportunity to watch and cheer. It was the most lavish and elaborate parade since the event's founding, filled with civic and society leaders and a long line of decorated carriages. Here the parade winds through the city along Main Street, looking north from the Temple Block. Note the spectators standing on buildings in front of office windows in order to get a better view of the festivities. (Title)

THE FIRST PROTESTANT CHURCH in Los Angeles was a unique, massive, Arizona-pink-sandstone
structure at 2000 South Figueroa Street that was
completed on March 23, 1896, with the Reverend
Burt Estes Howard as pastor. It occupied one-fourth
of a city block in what was then an area of large
handsome homes. Now the United University
Church at Hoover and Thirty-fourth Street, then it
was known as the First Presbyterian Church of Los
Angeles and was famous for many years for its
pipe organ and exceptional musical programs. The
church's members first organized in 1874, with Dr.
A. F. White as pastor, and in 1877 conducted
meetings in Good Templar's Hall. (Title)

THIS STRANGE-LOOKING STRUCTURE was
something out of *The Arabian Nights* when it was
built around the late 1890s in Venice. This hotel and
apartment house, located near the beach and ocean,
dominated the local skyline for many miles around,
and catered to a summertime resort crowd. Of Moorish architecture, the starkly white building was an
unusual sight to residents, who loved to point out
from passing vehicles its jutting towers, wide verandahs, and numerous spires. (Title)

CAHUENGA BOULEVARD back of Whitley Heights in the Hollywood Hills was just a trail leading into the mountains in 1897 when bicycle riders sometimes ventured out its way for picnics. Although
the area gained in popularity over the years, it wasn't until 1926 that Cahuenga was finally completed,
at a cost of $500,000, from Hollywood Boulevard to the San Fernando Valley. (Title)

EL ALISAL, the home of Charles F. Lummis from the 1890s to around 1920, was as colorful and different in its day as was Lummis himself. Lummis built his stone "castle" with his own hands, working for more than twenty years on it either as a carpenter or a mason. Using native rock, he put the house around a huge sycamore tree under which "Greek George" had camped with camels on his arrival in the Los Angeles area some sixty years earlier. Located in the Arroyo Seco near today's Pasadena, it stood in a grove of thirty sycamore trees, and was where Lummis worked and received his important visitors and guests. (Title)

THE FIRST GOLF CLUBHOUSE in Southern California was this windmill used by the Los Angeles "Windmill Links," whose twenty members taught themselves how to play by sinking some tomato cans in vacant lots at Pico and Alvarado boulevards. Afterwards, the club moved to Pico and Harvard in 1898 and was called the "Convent Links" because of its closeness to Immaculate Heart Convent.

IF THERE'S A WILL THERE'S A WAY: Sixty Los Angeles High School students who needed money for vacations on Santa Catalina Island in 1898 earned enough by picking apricots near Santa Paula, California. This picture shows part of the group, which became known as the "Gay Pickers of '98," in the apricot groves with their baskets. (Title)

THE CHARLES F. HARPER ESTATE in 1898 was located approximately at
Sunset and Laurel Canyon boulevards just south of the Hollywood Hills where
Laurel Canyon begins its run through the mountains north to the San Fernando
Valley. Harper, a pioneer hardware merchant, and his partner, R. H. Dalton,
opened an immediately prosperous hardware store in 1868 in the Allen Block at
Temple and Spring streets. (Title)

LOS ANGELES' FIRST TELEPHONE PAY STATION at 228 South Spring Street
in 1898 took care of the people who wanted to make local or long distance calls,
but who didn't own a telephone. It was operated by the Sunset Telephone Company, part of the Bell Telephone Company system, and had lines extending as far
as Salt Lake City and Portland, Oregon. Calls could be made to 40,000 other telephone owners, and rates varied as they do today, depending on the distance of the
call. Equipment reportedly was so crude, however, that it was almost impossible
to speak to someone in Salt Lake City. To talk to someone in San Francisco, the
rates were ¼ minute for 50 cents. Pictured in front of the station with the operator
was Roy Jillson, a messenger boy who later became a transmission operator. (H-E)

IN THE DAYS before Los Angeles was completely motorized, wide streets with
little traffic enabled the men and women wheelmen, as they were called, to go
for pleasure rides almost any time. Here at the corner of Figueroa Street and
Washington Boulevard in 1898 rides a fashionable matron of the day. Perhaps
trying to catch up, about a half block behind is another rider. (Title)

WIVES, SWEETHEARTS, FRIENDS, and other Angelenos cheered and waved Old Glory when the seventh regiment of California volunteers left Los Angeles from its armory at Eighth and Spring streets in 1898 for the Spanish-American War. The trip, however, was a disaster. The regiment suffered casualties, not in battle, but while at camp in the Presidio near San Francisco. Fevers bred by an unhealthy camp location took the lives of many valuable men, who were held in the camp for almost the entire length of the war. A granite statue which stood in the northeast corner of Pershing Square served as a memorial to the heroic young volunteers who were never given a chance to fight.

MISSION LIFE apparently agreed with some of its residents. For example, at the San Gabriel Mission, Eulalia Peres de Guilen, who claimed to be 140 years old, died in 1878. And when this picture was taken in 1898, Rogerio F. Rocha, a San Fernando Mission chorister and silversmith and the last of the San Fernando Mission Indians, reportedly was 95 years old and still strong enough to work in the fields. Rocha, who died in 1904, lived to be 103 years old, and here was gathering fruit of the cactus for food. (Title)

CALIFORNIA HOSPITAL, a four-story, fifty-bed, frame building at the corner of Hope and Fifteenth streets was opened on June 1, 1898. The hospital cost $30,000 to build, and was situated on a 330-foot site. Specially designed for medical research purposes and founded in 1887 by Dr. Walter Lindley, it was the third hospital to be established in Los Angeles County. (CHMC)

WHEN THE LOS ANGELES HIGH SCHOOL FOOTBALL TEAM of 1898 beat the University of Southern California, 6-0, it was probably the greatest upset in the history of the sport. The winning players were: (bottom row) Billy McIntosh, Dan Lawbesheimer, Jack Carson, George McDill, Phil Wilson, and Billy Edwards; (middle row) Frank Hutchins, Ernest W. Oliver, Stacey Catey, George Spence, Fred Engstrum, and Marshall Stimson; (top row) Roy Brousseau, Claude Friel, Israel Ludlow, Rollo Bidwell, Gay Lewis, and manager Harold Butler.

ABOUT ELEVEN YEARS after the first Hollywood lots began selling to the public in 1887, grading for a railroad took place along what is now Hollywood Boulevard. In those days of 1898, the streets were dirt roads lined with fruit trees and an occasional house. Actually, Hollywood was considered "way out" from the civic center, and not until the electric railway reached there did it get any attention from Angelenos. (Title)

THE FAMOUS LOS ANGELES HIGH SCHOOL "Kamera Klub" posed for this picture in 1899. First row, left to right: Ethel Wynn, John A. Moriarty, Lottie Brown, William Kessler, Alma Foy, Jack Marsh, Etta Janss, Annie Van Nuys, and Harry Gregory. Upper row, left to right: Florence Ganahl, Nell Deering, Fred Haines, Earle Anthony, Eugene R. Hallett, H. Stanley Benedict, and Robert Sibley. Members owned either a simple Eastman box camera or a more sophisticated type featuring a bellows that enabled the photographer to focus more precisely. After leaving school, some club members went on to become notable in Los Angeles society, business, and civic affairs. In any case, who took this picture? (SPNB)

THE CITY OF AVALON on Santa Catalina Island was a thriving community after its founding in 1887 by George R. Shatto. This was the view of its main street, Crescent Avenue, where the tourists used to buy various souvenirs and refreshments after coming off the boats. Note the Alonzo Wheeler bakery and coffee room, the Avalon Shell Store, the ice cream parlor which also sold candy, and the tents where people lived on the hill behind the stores. (Title)

THE START OF CONSTRUCTION of the breakwater for Los Angeles' harbor at San Pedro formally started in 1899 when 20,000 people from Los Angeles and the area around the port joined in a special celebration. This important event found the large crowd assembled near Point Fermin, where one of the barges loaded with rock lay ready for dumping. Plans had called for Pres. William McKinley to press an electrical button in the White House that would have tipped the barge and dumped the rock into the water. The connection didn't work, however, and the rock had to be pushed into the water by hand. Here, in 1899, trains begin bringing in the rock for the sea wall. (Title)

TERMINAL ISLAND BEACH at Los Angeles harbor, at the height of its glory in 1900, was a favorite swimming spot for many of Los Angeles' and Long Beach's wealthier residents. It was a stylish resort, one of the most fashionable on the Pacific Coast, with a bathhouse, a bar, and a restaurant, and was served by the Salt Lake Railroad which ran from Los Angeles to San Pedro, with stops in Long Beach and Terminal Island. Late in the 1920s, however, the beach and surrounding area were taken over by squatters who lived in shacks right at the water's edge. Eventually, after a bitter fight between the squatters and the City of Long Beach, the squatters were evicted, but Terminal Island never again regained its former popularity.

[68]

THIS GLASS-BOTTOM POWER LAUNCH did a lively business with tourists who were taken on a ride to Pebble Beach on South Catalina Island from Avalon around 1900. In addition to the glass-bottom boat, a bird farm was the island's principal attraction. Little by little, though, starting in 1887, Catalina became a favorite resort area, but it was years before there was patronage enough to warrant a daily steamer service. In 1887, the steamer *Falcon* left San Pedro for Catalina every seven or eight days, and returned the day after in time to catch the 3 p.m. train for Los Angeles. The fare was $4 for a round trip. (Title)

Into the Twentieth Century: 1900 to 1909

LOS ANGELES' MORE THAN 100,000 residents were so well established at the turn of the century that even real estate failures, dry seasons, and bank closings did little to impede their progress. Angelenos had proved that no matter what the failure, they could turn it around to an advantage, and that when things were really at their worst, they could celebrate and thumb their noses at disaster. As a result, Los Angeles started to grow with such vigor that it was obvious, even in the early 1900s, that it was destined to become one of the world's greatest cities.

Although the automobile had made its appearance before 1900, it wasn't until this decade that it was actually accepted. In the beginning, however, automobiles seemed such monsters that people who owned them couldn't even give them away. Instead, Angelenos remained faithful to their bicycles, and also began travelling on trolleys across the countryside in large numbers, on the extra-long, wide and speedy "Big Red Cars."

They royally welcomed Presidents William McKinley, William Howard Taft, and Theodore Roosevelt, brushed aside another financial panic, and sat back and waited for engineer William Mulholland to bring them water from the distant Owens Valley.

Boosters sold Los Angeles' climate to a shivering nation, and throughout the country promoted its mountains, beaches, fresh air, sunshine, and scenic wonders. An explosion of people responded, flooding Los Angeles from the East and the Midwest. Industries pushed out the orange groves, cities multiplied, and if California oranges didn't appear on every breakfast table in the nation, obviously something had to be wrong.

The face of the city was being uplifted. The first high-rise, constructed at Sixth and Main streets at a cost of $1,751,947, was nine stories high and boasted of a garden in the sky—on its roof, instead of on the ground.

There was no doubt in anyone's mind, as the decade drew to a close, that the former pueblo was growing up.

ONE OF THE FIRST GROUPS OF GOLFERS ever to play in Los Angeles is pictured posing in front of the Los Angeles Country Club when it was located at Pico Boulevard and Western Avenue in 1900. The photograph included Ed Tufts (far right with hat in hand), who was known in those days as the "father of golf" in Southern California. (H-E)

ONE OF LOS ANGELES' MOST ELEGANT HOMES in 1900 was the George Shatto residence on a hillside of Shatto Street (where the Good Samaritan Hospital now stands). It was the era of bric-a-brac and velvet and beads and lace curtains; every possible surface was covered with pictures and knickknacks. The transom over the door was colorfully stained glass, and the elaborate ceiling was the ultimate in beauty—yet the chairs were uncomfortable, with stiff backs and a minimum of upholstery. George R. Shatto was a pioneer realty developer who purchased Catalina Island in 1887, founded the town of Avalon, and built the Metropole Hotel there. After his death, his wife Clara carried on developing Lafayette Park, which she gave to the city; she donated the site of the First Congregational Church, which at one time stood at Sixth and Hoover streets; and subdivided Orange Heights, an area bounded by Third and Hoover streets, Vermont Avenue, and Wilshire Boulevard. Mrs. Shatto died in 1942 at age eighty-nine in her home in Beverly Hills. (Title)

THE HOME of Geronimo Lopez and his wife, Catalina, in 1900 was located in the city of San Fernando at the corner of Maclay Avenue and Pico Street. Lopez, a pioneer San Fernando Valley businessman, was at the signing of the Treaty of Cahuenga, which ended the Mexican-American War of 1846-47, and which placed California under American rule. He was the valley's first postmaster, and owned the area's first general store. On the balcony of their home are, left to right, Aurelia, the Lopez' maid; George Millen, a family friend; Stephen N. Lopez, Geronimo's son; Celeste Lopez, Geronimo's daughter; and Sarah Lopez-Britton, another daughter. (SPNB)

EVEN IN THE EARLY PART of the twentieth century, Los Angeles was known for the "characters" that roamed its streets. This famous old-timer, a familiar sight on Main Street in 1900, finally disappeared without leaving a trace. Taken at Main and Temple streets, the photograph shows the Baker Block tower in the right background. (H-E)

POMONA'S CITIZENS were ready to support their city council and even fight to keep outsiders from interfering with a franchise to the Salt Lake Railroad, now the Union Pacific, in 1901. Men who didn't have rifles carried clubs. Here they waited during the night to stop any troublemakers from entering their city. Note that almost all the men wore badges, and those who weren't lawmen had probably been sworn in as deputies. (Danning)

EASTLAKE PARK was a placid and tranquil place where even the ladies could go for a rowboat ride in the early 1900s. The property was purchased for park use by Los Angeles from the Southern Pacific Railroad Company for $448.64. The land was originally donated to the railroad for a depot, but proved unsuitable. After the city acquired the property, now part of Boyle Heights between Mission Road and Alhambra Avenue, it was improved with lawns, trees, shrubs, flowers, and a small lake. In 1911, when the Los Angeles Board of Park Commissioners ordered additional improvements, a bathhouse and pavilion were constructed and the landscaping was changed. (Title)

LOS ANGELES TENNIS PLAYERS were a fashionable crew in the early 1900s. In this formally posed picture, the men wore blazers, schoolboy-type caps, and long trousers. The women wore striped shirtwaists with straw brimmed hats. Although tennis clothes have changed drastically over the years, the racquets and balls basically are the same as those used today. (Title)

ONE OF THE MOST BEAUTIFUL HOMES in Southern California was the Paul de Longpre residence in Hollywood. De Longpre, a famous artist who exhibited his first flower canvas at the Paris Salon in 1876, gained a reputation for painting only flowers and liberally decorated his home with his work. His house, which was built in 1901, was one of the showplaces of the West. Note the staircase and banister, the rugs used as decorations on floors and walls, the ceiling and its many electric light bulbs, and the colorfully covered chairs and cloth portieres. (Title)

ANGEL'S FLIGHT, a popular landmark in downtown Los Angeles for sixty-eight years, was opened in 1901 on Third Street between Hill and Olive. Special ceremonies took place, including a speech by Mayor M. F. Snyder; ladies of Olive Heights served punch to notables. Two cars, "Olivet" and "Sinai," hauled passengers up and down a sharp incline. When one car went up, the other came down, both meeting about midway on the 33-percent rise. Cost of a one-way ride was one cent until 1953, when the price rose to two rides for a nickel. The builder of the one-block railroad, which served residents of Bunker Hill, was Col. J. W. Eddy, a prominent businessman. (H-E)

This isn't Angel's Flight, it's the COURT FLIGHT.

OSTRICHES WERE FIRST INTRODUCED to Angelenos about 1885, when Dr. Sketchley, a naturalist, opened up a successful farm and coach service that connected with the end of the Temple Street cable car line. He then moved to Red Bluff, where he failed and lost everything. Soon after, in 1887, Edwin Cawston shipped a load of ostriches from South Africa to Los Angeles. Many died on the way over, but forty survived. Cawston *(right),* shown in this picture plucking a male ostrich, opened a farm at Washington Gardens, and later transferred it to La Habra. In 1908, he moved again, this time setting up his ostriches between Los Angeles and Pasadena on the Los Feliz ranch near where Glendale is today. (Title)

PRES. WILLIAM McKINLEY visited Los Angeles in 1901, accompanied by his wife, and rode in a flower-decorated carriage in the La Fiesta parade. Just two months later he would be assassinated by an anarchist by the name of Leon Czolgosz.

CALIFORNIA HOSPITAL, known by 1902 as the largest and best-equipped hospital west of Chicago, was owned and operated by physicians and surgeons. In fact, the hospital physicians comprised almost half of the staff of the University of Southern California's School of Medicine during those years. (CHMC)

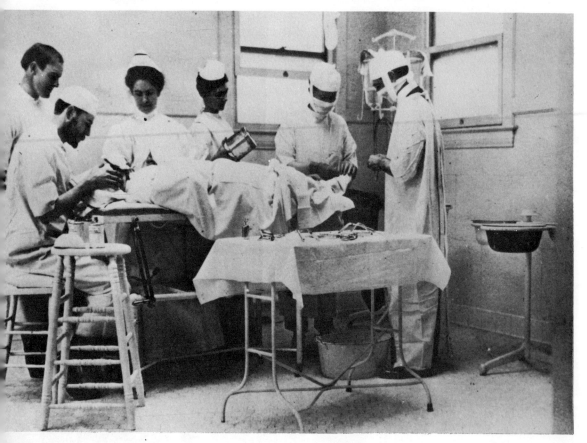

[74]

ONE OF THE FEW ATTRACTIONS for tourists around the turn of the century was horse racing at Ascot Park, which was located "far out" from the city in what today is south-central Los Angeles. The park, run by the Los Angeles Jockey Club in the early 1900s, constantly battled with citizens who opposed gambling, and who eventually caused its demise. (CSAF)

THE FIRST FOOTBALL GAME in Rose Bowl history, billed as an East-West contest, took place on January 1, 1902, in Pasadena's Tournament Park. The University of Michigan beat Stanford easily, 49-0. There were only seats for about one thousand, but 8,500 jammed into the park, breaking down fences to gain entrance. Michigan's famous "Point-A-Minute" team, coached by Fielding H. Yost *(right)*, paraded in the 1902 celebrations, and then went into the pits with noseguards on its old-fashioned helmets and mass interference behind its runner *(below)* that would be illegal today. (CSAF-SPNB)

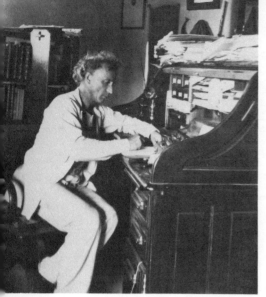

NONCONFORMIST, COLORFUL, character, eccentric, and showman were all words used to describe Charles Fletcher Lummis, who also was a gifted writer, historian-researcher, newspaper reporter, librarian, and magazine and newspaper editor in the late 1800s and early 1900s. Lummis established himself with Los Angeles citizens in 1884 by hiking, "for fun and study," 3,507 miles in 143 days from Cincinnati to Los Angeles, writing breezy stories for the *Los Angeles Times* while on his walk. His experiences were later published in his first book, *A Tramp Across the Continent.* He followed *Tramp* with books about the Southwest, about Spanish America from Colorado to Chile, and with Indian folk stories. He helped found the Southwest Museum in 1907, and was instrumental in the restoration of many Southland missions that were neglected and decaying. In 1915, in recognition of his historical work, the King of Spain conferred upon Lummis the "Knight Commander of the Royal Order of Ysabel la Catolica." (Title)

WHEN MARTIN BEKINS and his Bekins Van and Storage Company moved to Los Angeles from Sioux City, Iowa, in 1895, he rented an office at Fourth Street and Alameda Avenue, and used the rooms behind the office as his living quarters. Although his horse-drawn van was a familiar sight around the city, his two trucks that operated on two-cylinder, air-cooled engines became even more popular when introduced in 1903. The horse-drawn vans were phased out in 1918.

FIRST PRIZE in the La Fiesta parade contest in 1903, the year the *Los Angeles Examiner* was founded with R. A. Farrelly as its first managing editor, went to these ladies who represented the Chamber of Commerce. It was the year, too, in which Pres. Theodore Roosevelt came to review the parade. (Title)

WHEN THE PACIFIC COAST BASEBALL LEAGUE started up in 1903, Los Angeles entered this team which won the league championship under manager and owner, Jim Morley, center. The team won 133 games and lost 78 over a long season which stretched from late March through October. Los Angeles won additional championships in 1905, 1907, and 1908, and for many years thereafter was one of the strongest franchises on the Pacific Coast. (CSAF)

THE HOLLYWOOD HOTEL between Highland and Orchid Avenue was a large, quiet, country resort in 1903 when it opened under the ownership of a subdivider who used the hotel to put up people who might buy lots in the middle of lemon groves sitting along the foothills of the Santa Monica Mountains. The movies, however, made it famous. Every big name in the industry at one time or another was a guest, and Rudolph Valentino, who was married there, remained for a honeymoon. To get to the hotel in the early 1900s, visitors had to wind along Hollywood Boulevard, which was only a sandy trail lined with fruit trees, or ride two hours from Los Angeles by trolley past open countryside, orchards, and farm houses. (Ronnie)

OLD CABLE LINES at First Street and Broadway were torn up in 1903 to make way for Henry E. Huntington's Pacific Electric Railway, which became known later as the "Big Red Cars." At their peak, the electric trolleys were the finest and largest interurban cars in the world. Huntington began with twenty miles of track, and eventually ran some 1,163 miles. Success was due to easy access by riders and the speed of the cars, which generally hit 40 miles per hour, and sometimes 60 miles per hour. In 1949, when the buses and automobiles monopolized the streets, the electric trolleys were discontinued.

[78]

FEW PEOPLE COULD RESIST the colorful poppies as they rode through Altadena on the trolley in 1904. The poppies were so attractive that the conductor was forced to stop so that passengers could pick bouquets. Altadena, north of Pasadena, was located at the base of the Sierra Madre Mountains on a mesa 1,100 to 2,000 feet above sea level. On a clear day, residents could see portions of Los Anglees, the Pacific Ocean, and even Catalina Island. (Title)

LOS ANGELES WENT OIL CRAZY around the turn of the century after oil was discovered in a residential area by Edward Laurence Doheny. Three fields suddenly sprouted, stretching within a long, narrow strip less than half a mile wide which bordered on downtown Los Angeles and which extended to Vermont Avenue. At the height of the oil drilling in the early 1900s, some 1150 wells, almost one on top of the other, dotted the landscape. Homeowners literally went mad for the black gold, putting up wells in back yards, in gardens, and on lawns. In many cases, homes were moved so that there would be even more space for additional derricks. (Title)

FISHERMEN who lived off the sea built their homes right on the sand at the foot of the palisades in Redondo Beach in 1904, and took their chances with the waves. When storms struck, the homes would be demolished, and the fishermen would have to put up new ones. The one advantage was that they could be on the job in minutes. (Title)

LOS ANGELES was the nation's first city to recognize the importance of municipal playgrounds by establishing the first city department of recreation in 1904. When its first facility, the Violet Street playground, opened in 1905 at 2017 Violet Street, it was such an unusual event that children rushed to play on its equipment, and parents followed along to watch. (H-E)

ABBOTT KINNEY envisioned a new city on the tide-flats and lagoons south of Ocean Park, and in 1900 Norman F. Marsh and C. H. Russell came up with its design. Three years later, to get sufficient money to pay for his dream, Kinney sold off all of his important Los Angeles holdings and purchased enough acreage on which to build his city. In 1905, Kinney's city, called the "Venice of America," opened with much hoopla, featuring canals; high-arching foot bridges; Italian singing gondoliers who poled gondolas imported from Italy; ornate arcades; an elegant hotel, St. Mark's, which was the exact copy of one in Venice, Italy; and a restaurant in the shape of a Spanish galleon. In 1906, Kinney added side shows, carnival-type concessions, and joy rides. Today, the days of glory are past and only the canals and foot bridges remain as reminders of a once colorful past. (Title)

ONE YEAR AFTER Ocean Park was incorporated as a city in 1904, a building boom in the South-land hit the beach city. A bathhouse was constructed at a cost of $185,000, and a pier and auditorium for dancing were built. By 1905, Ocean Park was so popular as a beach resort that as many as 100,000 persons would squeeze into the area on holidays. (Bayrd)

MacARTHUR PARK, formerly Westlake Park, always has been a popular recreational spot for Los Angeles citizens. The park was built in 1885 when Mayor William H. Workman ordered new topsoil, had trees and shrubs planted, and filled a ravine with water to create a lake. Eventually a pavilion was built, a rental rowboat service started, and the park was connected to downtown Los Angeles when the electric railway was extended to it in 1898. By 1905, the park was basically the same as it stands today at Wilshire Boulevard and Alvarado Street, except that tall office buildings and hotels now surround it. In 1905, an oil field stood west of the park, and derricks could be seen poking up above the mansion-like homes in the background. (Title)

MAIN STREET from Fourth looking north in 1905 showed a busy time dominated by streetcars, carriages, and bicycle riders. A few blocks further north, at Temple and Main, a committee of citizens led by Joseph Mesmer purchased the famous Downey Block in 1905 and presented it to the government for a site of the proposed Federal Building. The same year, to locate closer to the business activity, the Farmers and Merchants National Bank moved to Fourth and Main from Commercial and Main. Note the changing style, with awnings jutting out from windows of the office buildings. (Title)

THE FIRST STORE, a grocery, opened in Hollywood in 1905, and prospered as the community boomed along with the movie industry, which was just beginning to flex its muscles. Located on the northeast corner of Cahuenga Avenue and Sunset Boulevard, this grocery was famous for carrying everything from soup to nuts. (Title)

[83]

THE FIRST FLIGHT of a dirigible in the Southern California area took place in 1905 when Thomas Scott Baldwyn flew his airship *Bullet* at Playa del Rey. Scott brought his dirigible down from Oakland where he had built it in 1892. At first it was run with a bicycle pedal and a propeller, but when it couldn't be controlled, Baldwyn installed an automobile engine in 1892, and finally flew it in a guided flight in 1904. The dirigible was sold to the government in 1908, and was the first airship owned by the United States. (SPNB)

HOLLYWOOD at the corner of Franklin Avenue near Bronson about 1905 was a sleepy, undeveloped place with a few homes and palm trees, fruit orchards, and farms. Like the rest of the Southland, it was a waterless area with a dry gully, as the picture shows. Except for an occasional horse and wagon, there was little activity over its bridges and dirt roads. (Title)

LOS ANGELES' LOVE AFFAIR with its beaches began in the 1880s and has continued through the years right up to the present time. Sunbathing and swimming, of course, were the two logical activities, but the more obvious one turned out to be the bathing beauty contest. Here in 1906 were the finalists of a contest held in Venice. Apparently, in those days, there was more to their beauties than met the eye! (SPNB)

THE GANG AT THE TRANSCONTINENTAL FREIGHT STATION in Los Angeles took time out to pose in 1906, just after the fourth outlet from Los Angeles to the East Coast had been opened through the Salt Lake Railroad. (II-E)

THIS WAS THE STAFF of the Los Angeles High School when it was located at 451 North Hill Street in 1907. Prof. William Housh was principal, and Mrs. Susan B. Dorsey, who later became superintendent of schools, was vice principal. On the staff, too, was Mrs. Chloe Jones, an English instructor who served earlier as the first woman superintendent of schools from 1880 to 1881. The school was constructed in 1890 at a cost of $70,000. It was a four-story red brick building, contained forty rooms, and had 400 students. As Los Angeles grew, the school expanded, and a fourteen-room annex was erected on property across the street on the east side of Hill. It moved in 1917 to its present site, Olympic Boulevard and Rimpau Avenue, where it started with 1,937 students. (Title)

Daily Bulletin
LOS ANGELES POLICE DEPARTMENT

CHIEF'S OFFICE   SEPTEMBER 9, 1908   NO. 550

Arrest For Murder

CARL D. SUTHERLAND, aged about 25 years; 5-7; 135 lbs.; heavy head of brown hair, which is worn long and parted on the side; medium complexion; smooth shaven; gray eyes. May be dressed in brown coat and pants, light colored soft hat. IS PROBABLY WOUNDED, having left a trail of blood behind him. Painter by occupation.

At about 9:30 o'clock a. m., September 9, 1908, this man shot Captain W. H. Auble, of this Department, three times while the Captain was attempting to arrest him at 9th and Grand avenue, inflicting fatal injuries.

Sutherland had been living at 337 Georgia street with a pal. Take no chances.

EDWARD KERN,
CHIEF OF POLICE

THE DAILY BULLETIN of the Los Angeles Police Department in 1908 called for the arrest of Carl D. Sutherland, who shot and killed Capt. W. H. Auble while the captain was trying to arrest him at Ninth Street and Grand Avenue. Sutherland committed suicide after the murder, and left a confession, which was found nineteen years later under a Glendale house. (H-E)

BURBANK'S FIRST SAVINGS INSTITUTION was the Burbank State Bank, which opened in 1908. It later became Security-First National Bank in the same location on the southwest corner of Olive Avenue and San Fernando Boulevard. (SPNB)

THIS RAMBLER MOTOR TRUCK was the first piece of motorized equipment for fire departments on the Pacific Coast when it was purchased in 1907 by Long Beach. The city at that time bought two trucks to modernize its all-horse-drawn equipment. Behind the driver's seat was a forty-gallon chemical tank and a metal basket that carried 500 feet of fire hose. By 1914, Long Beach's Fire Department had become completely motorized, and had retired its seven horses.

HOLLYWOOD'S ANNUAL TILTING TOURNAMENT and flower-show parade, viewed from sidewalks and grandstands by more than 20,000 persons in 1908, was composed of floats, automobiles, equestrians, carriages, and pony carts that carried the area's social, civic, business, and political leaders. Typical of the occasion is this flower-decorated automobile driven by Harold Stern, with Lillian Grass next to him. In the rear, at left, is Eulalie Grass, with Elsie Stern in the middle. The other girl was not identified. (Title)

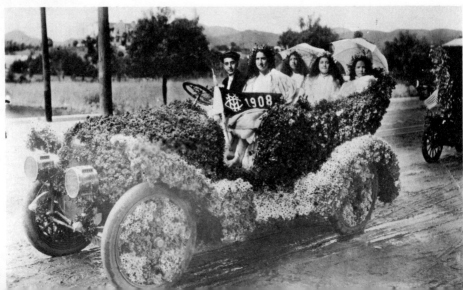

LEADING OFF the 1909 Tournament of Roses parade in Pasadena was this herald, who was the center of attention on her flower-decorated horse. A special attraction that year was Ezra Meeker and his oxcart. Meeker, a pioneer traveler who crossed the continent with an ox team over the old Oregon Trail in 1852, had repeated the trip in 1906. E. W. Knowlton decorated his surrey with 500 American Beauty roses, and Walter Raymond decorated his automobile in the shape of a huge seashell. (Title)

[87]

CHARIOT RACES were held from 1905 to 1915 as part of the Tournament of Roses in Tournament Park at Wilson Avenue and California Street. The races were billed as exciting, dangerous action, and reached a peak in 1908 when a driver named Michel dueled C. C. West in the final heat. They were neck and neck down the stretch with West on the inside near the rail when near the finish line, Michel cut in front of West's team and knocked down two of West's horses. Judges declared West the winner on a foul. (Title)

THE "FIRST TRACKLESS TROLLEY IN AMERICA" was how this Laurel Canyon Express to Bungalowtown was billed in 1910. The trolleys ran for five years from the intersection of Laurel Canyon and Sunset boulevards to Bungalowtown, a real estate development nestled in the hills. For ten cents, passengers could take a scenic ride through the hills, up grades as high as 12 percent and at speeds ranging from four to twenty-five miles per hour. Service was offered every half hour from 7:45 a.m. to 11:15 p.m. Since there was only one pair of overhead wires, the operator of the downward-bound car had to remove his contactors from the wires when the upward-bound car approached. (H-E)

THE LOBBY of the YMCA building in downtown Los Angeles was one of the most popular meeting places in the city around 1910. Convenient to most of the area, it was where members went throughout the years for inexpensive and clean accommodations, for the use of its gymnasium and physical fitness equipment, and for its meeting rooms. The building was torn down in 1969, but during its lifetime was considered an architectural masterpiece. (YMCA)

Stars are Born: 1910 to 1919

BY 1910, LOS ANGELES found itself populated with a flourishing 320,000 persons who were about to embark on one of the city's most exciting periods, centering around Hollywood, which was born earlier, but which in this decade actually went through its childhood to become known world-wide for its films and stars. Movie-making captured the imagination of the public like no other industry.

Leading the way was Mary Pickford, who first started working for $5 a day, and who later made millions when she became "America's Sweetheart." But Mary wasn't the only star. Others behind the scene and in front of the cameras included D. W. Griffith, Thomas H. Ince, Mack Sennett, Jesse L. Lasky, Cecil B. DeMille, Charlie Chaplin, Carl Laemmle, Tom Mix, Hoot Gibson, Douglas Fairbanks, Irving Thalberg, and Louis B. Mayer.

Along with the movie stars came the much-needed water which began flowing into Los Angeles from the Owens River Aqueduct. It was needed desperately by so many other cities nearby that residents of those areas were happy to let Los Angeles annex them, just to get water, even if they had to assume part of Los Angeles' bonded indebtedness.

More oil was discovered, and it seemed as if the city was floating on one vast, never-ending pool. Black gold poured from Rancho La Merced, Huntington Beach, Long Beach, Torrance, Baldwyn Hills, Venice, El Segundo, and Wilmington, and there was no end in sight.

Angelenos, who had never seen an airplane fly, suddenly saw a great many at the Dominguez Air Meet. They watched and cheered and yelled as Glen Curtiss made the first powered flight in the West, and went wild as others set numerous flying records right in front of their eyes. As a result, Angelenos went aviation-crazy, and such individuals as Curtiss, Glenn L. Martin, Donald W. Douglas, Allen and Malcolm Loughhead (Lockheed), and John K. Northrop began manufacturing airplanes to meet the demand.

The San Fernando Valley doubled the size of the city when it was annexed, all 108,732 acres, and the famous Hollywood Bowl was born where spectators sat on the hillsides and brushed away ants.

Then came World War I. Angelenos contributed to Liberty Loan drives, fasted on meatless days, ate wheatless meals, cut down on the use of oil, registered for the draft, and women took over for the men who left to fight in Europe. Although the city had given up much of its manpower to the holocaust, its population continued to climb, and thus set the stage for the biggest boom yet.

ABOUT 35,000 PERSONS watched the greatest of French aviators, Louis Paulhan, take off from in front of the grandstand during the 1910 Dominguez Field air meet. Paulhan, in his Farnham biplane, thrilled the huge crowd by flying to Arcadia and back in 1 hour, 2 minutes, and 42 4/5 seconds. (CSAF)

DIRIGIBLES as well as planes excited the huge crowds that attended the Dominguez Field international aviation meet in 1910 as they raced each other through the skies. To make a dirigible rise or descend, its pilot had to run forward or back on the framework below the gas bag. The meet, which lasted from January 10 to January 20, drew 50,000 persons on some days, and was probably the first air demonstration ever held. (Title)

[91]

WHEN THE COUNTRY'S first air meet was held in a barley field at Dominguez Rancho south of Compton in 1910, California Hospital established the first emergency aviation hospital at the field under the direction of Miss Ann Williamson (left). The portable cottage was equipped with an operating table, and a horse-drawn California Hospital ambulance. (CHMC)

A LOS ANGELES FIRE DEPARTMENT band serenaded residents in front of the Los Angeles Evening Herald Building around 1911, when the newspaper was owned by William Randolph Hearst. It was located at 128 South Broadway until 1925, when its presses, which for years had entertained thousands of persons who watched them operate behind the glass windows, were moved into larger quarters at 1243 South Trenton Street. A branch office remained, but it too finally needed more space and moved in 1930. In 1931, Hearst purchased the *Los Angeles Evening Express* and merged it with the *Evening Herald,* creating the *Los Angeles Herald-Express.* (H-E)

[92]

FOSSILS HAVE BEEN FOUND in the La Brea Tar Pits ever since 1895 when William Denton came up with a sabre-toothed cat's tooth. But not until Prof. W. W. Orcutt, a Union Oil Company geologist prospecting on La Brea Rancho in 1905, discovered other fossils was any attention paid to the finds. The pits' main excavations, under the shadow of Salt Lake Oil Field derricks, however, were made from 1906 to 1913 by Occidental College and Los Angeles High School, and from 1913 to 1915 by the Museum of Natural History. The museum came up with the most bones, some 500,000 that included the remains of emperor mammoths, giant ground sloths, dire wolves, saber-toothed tigers, birds, mastadons, imperial elephants, short-faced bears, and bison, proving that more than a half million years ago, Los Angeles was really the Wild, Wild West. (SPNB)

THE FIRST CARGO SHIP to be built by the Craig Shipyard in 1911 at the port of Long Beach was launched with these people attending the ceremony. The man with his left hand in his pocket and plaid vest is John Craig, owner of the shipyard, and to his right is a Long Beach pioneer, Jotham Bixby. (LB)

BURBANK CITY LOTS were sold in 1887 with great enthusiasm and advertising that claimed "Land and ocean, mountain and valley, sunshine and shade, offer here their choicest benefactions to prolong the lives of the feeble and enhance the enjoyment of the robust." By 1911, when the city was incorporated, Burbank's downtown, looking north on San Fernando Boulevard from Angeleno Street, was used to traffic that was a mixture of the horse and the automobile. The livery stable and feed store were typical of the time, but the garage and real estate office hint of progress that was to come. (SPNB)

LOS ANGELES POLICE DEPARTMENT officers were so happy to be motorized in 1911 that they eagerly posed in their autos in front of the old Central Police Station on First Street for this picture. The officers were (1) Roy Walls, (3) Lieutenant Mathieson, (4) Officer Johnson, (5) Detective William Moore, (6) Charley Block, (7) Sergeant Bill Hackett, and (8) William Drogemeir. No. 2 was George Fisher, the driver of the first car. (Whitehead)

WHEN HOLLYWOOD was still in its infancy in 1911, the Six Mile House, also known as the Blondeau Tavern, was the home of the Nestor film company, first motion picture studio in Hollywood, located at the northeast corner of Sunset Boulevard and Gower Avenue. One of the firm's first films was a "Mutt and Jeff" comedy, produced by Al Christie, who in 1917 formed his own Christie Film Company. Picture making actually started in the Southern California area around 1907 when independent companies escaped New York City and fought the "Trust," the Motion Picture Patents Company which controlled the movie industry, and came to Los Angeles for year-round sunshine and terrain variety. Within the year, however, the Nestor company became affiliated with Carl Laemmle, Sr., and the Universal Film Manufacturing Company was formed. (Alcana)

VAN NUYS GREW so fast from the time of its inception in February 1911, that by December lots were selling like hotcakes. What contributed to its phenomenal growth was the Pacific Electric Railway's extension to it on December 11, 1911, and establishment of daily service. On that day, people from throughout the Southland poured into the town to see what the fuss was all about. Fares on the Pacific Electric were forty-five cents one way from Los Angeles, and seventy-five cents round trip. Note the land-tract office and the crowd waiting for "free" literature on the left. (H-E)

DON GERONIMO LOPEZ and his wife, Catalina, posed in 1911 with their family on the day of their sixtieth wedding anniversary at their home in the city of San Fernando. Geronimo is sitting third from left in the second row, with Catalina to his right. The Lopez family consisted of thirteen children, nine daughters and four boys. Geronimo and Catalina in this period of their life spent a lot of time rocking on their front porch. Geronimo, however, sometimes went horseback riding to the San Fernando Mission, while Catalina sewed and mended clothes for the family at home. At Christmas time, Geronimo also liked dressing up like Santa Claus for the children. Catalina died in 1918, and Geronimo in 1921. (Title)

WHEN THE FIRST SHIP, the S.S. *Iqua,* entered the new municipal port at Long Beach on June 2, 1911, it was a surprise to everyone. As a result, city officials decided they would royally greet the next ship to arrive. When the S. S. *Santa Barbara* docked on June 24, 1911, carrying 350,000 board feet of Oregon pine, bands played and a few hundred persons turned out. Mayor Charles H. Windham was so anxious to be the first on board that he had himself hoisted to the deck by way of the freighter's cargo hook. (LB)

MAX FACTOR'S third store, this small establishment at Third and Hill streets, became a "hangout" for the movie stars in 1912. Factor (left), with his sons who worked after school and on Saturdays, had specialized in make-up and hair goods for the theatrical professions since 1908. California's pioneer manufacturer of cosmetics and perfumes, he started distributing his products nationally in 1927, and world-wide in 1930. In addition to coming up with more make-up "firsts" than any other cosmetician in history, Factor filled the biggest hair-goods order in Hollywood history, creating 10,000 wigs and hair pieces for the movie, *The Ten Commandments.* (Alcana)

THE BEVERLY HILLS HOTEL, when it opened its doors in 1912, sat surrounded by bean fields and little else. Since there were no hangouts for the early Hollywood settlers in those days, the hotel provided the room, a lobby with a blazing fire and a bar. With such an inducement, the likes of W. C. Fields, John Barrymore, Gene Fowler, and Will Rogers regularly left the nearby hills and canyons to seek sustenance here. (Fraggi)

MANHATTAN BEACH was a small, growing city that had to struggle against constantly shifting sands in 1912, the year it received its charter. As a result, its boardwalks moved, and it was useless to attempt to pave the streets. The three main buildings that year, looking at the city center, were (1) the Neptune Club, (2) the real estate office, and (3) the city hall. (SPNB)

DEAN BARTLETT CROMWELL, who during his lifetime at the University of Southern California was hailed as the "Maker of Champions," was the football coach of this YMCA team in 1912. Later, Cromwell would win eleven NCAA track and field championships, more than any other coach ever, and would coach the United States to a track and field victory in the 1948 Olympics in London. During his career, which ended in 1962 when he died at the age of eighty-two, he produced eight Olympic champions who won twelve Olympic gold medals between them. (YMCA)

BLANCHE STUART SCOTT, the first American woman aviator—and "Mistress of the Air" until she quit flying in 1916—was known for taking chances and running risks by the time she performed at the 1912 Dominguez Field air meet. Described as a dainty little miss with rosy, dimpled cheeks, she was a sorority girl from Rochester who was taught to fly in 1910 by Glenn Curtiss at Hammondsport, New York, after she had smashed the world's record in an automobile dash from New York City to San Francisco. Here she poses in the contraption she flew in the 1912 Los Angeles meet. Miss Scott never acquired a flying license. "It would have been too difficult to pass the test." she reportedly said. (Title)

PHILLIP PARMALEE, one of the more prominent of the California aviators, entertained a lineup of spectators at the 1912 Dominguez Field air meet. Parmalee was second in money won in the competition and on one flight performed three figure-eights in 1 minute, 2 3/5 seconds. The aviator also flew Wright gliders such as this one. Parmalee, taught how to fly by Orville Wright in 1910 in Dayton, Ohio, met his death soon after this Dominguez meet while flying in an exhibition in Washington. (Title)

THE FORMAL OPENING of the Los Angeles Athletic Club in 1912 was one of the great social events of the day. Highlighting the occasion were William May Garland (right), club vice president, and Frank Garbutt, club president, next to him. Located on Seventh Street near Olive, the club boasted of the first swimming pool ever to be built on the upper floor of a building.

WATER CAME to Los Angeles in 1913 over an aqueduct which started in 1908 in the Owens Valley, and which ended some three hundred miles later in the San Fernando Valley above Sylmar. The project comprised 142 separate tunnels which totaled 53 miles; 12 miles of inverted steel siphons from seven to eleven feet wide; 24 miles of open, unlined conduit; 39 miles of open, cement conduit; and 97 miles of covered conduit. Teams of fifty-two mules were used to haul single sections of the large pipe into position. After it was completed, not one pump had to be used to bring water the entire distance, from a height of 3,800 feet above sea level to 3,000 feet. Its engineer, William Mulholland *(right),* who also was the first superintendent of the Los Angeles Water Department, poured cement for the aqueduct according to an ancient Roman formula. In addition, Mulholland devised an ingenious system of hydraulic sluicing, which later was adopted in the construction of the Panama Canal. Mulholland died in 1935, after serving the people of Los Angeles for more than fifty years. (Title-LADWP)

LOS ANGELES NEVER WOULD have grown to its present size and wealth if water hadn't been brought into the city from the Owens Valley. Here, on November 5, 1913, a huge crowd turned out to witness the first flow from the north at the Cascades above Sylmar in the San Fernando Valley. As the foaming liquid roared down and filled the aqueduct, Los Angeles Water Department engineer William Mulholland, speaking to the crowd, said, "There it is—take it!" (SPNB)

SUSAN B. DORSEY became the first famous woman educator when she was appointed assistant superintendent of schools for Los Angeles in 1913. Shown are, left to right, John Francis, superintendent of schools; Edwin Markham, the famous poet who wrote "The Man With the Hoe;" and Mrs. Dorsey. Mrs. Dorsey held her position for seven years, and in 1920 was promoted to superintendent of schools, a job she held for nine years. (Alcana)

A FIRE in Los Angeles in 1913 was a great spectacle, as much as it is today, and spectators would rush to the scene in order to view the event. This fire took place at the corner of Third Street and Broadway, facing north. Since fire safety rules were nonexistent, and fire prevention wasn't pushed until 1916, it was imperative that the firemen get to the fire as quickly as possible, in order to prevent thousands of dollars worth of damage to other properties. (Title)

ROAD RACES in the early 1900s were conducted in what are now the beach areas of Santa Monica, Venice, and West Los Angeles, and over the Speedway, a street which still exists at the ocean between the Marina del Rey harbor entrance and Navy Street at the city of Santa Monica. In addition to the Speedway, the route, which would be lined by thousands of spectators, included Santa Monica, Wilshire, San Vicente, and Venice boulevards. In this race in 1914, one of the cars scoots under an overpass from which race officials and other observers are watching. (Alcana)

LOS ANGELES FIREMEN relaxed in 1915 by playing cards and by practicing on their musical instruments. However, at any time they might have been called to dash to a fire. This was the station house of Engine Company No. 23 and Truck Company No. 5. The arrow points to Ralph J. Scott, who was appointed chief in 1919. Obviously, the kibitzing in such close quarters was kept to a minimum. (LAFD)

[102]

THE MUNICIPAL DISTRIBUTION of electricity began in Los Angeles when, with ceremonies to mark the occasion, the first pole was erected at Pasadena Avenue (North Figueroa Street) and Piedmont Street on March 30, 1916. The organization that became the Los Angeles Department of Water and Power started delivering electricity to a few hundred customers, but did not at that time have its own power plant, buying its first electrical energy from Pasadena, instead. The city's San Francisquito Canyon Power Plant No. 1, which started operating in April 1917, was its first. (LADWP)

CECIL B. DeMILLE (right) became interested in flying when the United States declared war on Germany in 1917. He was too old for military service at thirty-six, but the Army Air Corps was so desperate for fliers that it said, if he would learn how to fly, he would get his commission. Tony Lynch (left), a pilot, and Al Wilson, another pilot, taught DeMille how, but the war ended and the director-producer never got his commission. Here with Lynch and DeMille in front of their Jenny on Culver Field in 1917 is Jeannie MacPherson. (Locklear)

A SPAD, A FOKKER D-VII, and an SE-5 paraded down Broadway on their way to DeMille Field No. 1 in 1918. The field was located on forty acres at the southwest corner of Crescent Avenue (now Fairfax) and Melrose Avenue. The planes were exhibited the following day during the celebration, "A Day at the Western Front." (DeMille)

THE MERCURY AVIATION COMPANY, organized by Cecil B. DeMille, boasted of having the top
pilots in the world in 1919. They included a girl, Jeannie MacPherson (standing third from right); Ben
Heflinger, the airport superintendent (third from left in front row), and Wayne Alles, director of sales
(fifth from left in front row). David E. Thompson, the company's chief pilot, is standing fourth from
right. (Locklear)

[104]

THE YEAR WORLD WAR I ENDED, the San Fernando Valley, north of what today is Ventura Boulevard in the Van Nuys area, already was showing signs of becoming the crowded community it is now.
Although most of the valley was still open and flowing, flat farm land, a new building boom would
soon pick up where it left off before the outbreak of the war in Europe in 1914. (Title)

The hell you say! This is SANTA MARIA, CAL. c. 1920 - 1st Nat'l Bank is blt. Bk of Silva is wht

SCREEN ACTRESS MARY PICKFORD, "America's Sweetheart," became "Honorary Ace of the Air Service" in special Memorial Day ceremonies conducted by Air Service officers at DeMille Field No. 2 in 1919. The day's program, billed as "A Day at the Western Front," featured flying exhibitions and stunts, and displays of aircraft under the command of a then-young colonel, "Hap" Arnold. Jimmy Doolittle, another young officer of the day, was the leader of a five-plane Ream Field army stunt team. Other stars who attended included Gloria Swanson, Donald Crisp, Bryant Washburn, Douglas Fairbanks, Wanda Holly, and Charlie Chaplin. (DeMille)

THE FIRST COMPANY to fly passengers and newspapers from Long Beach to Catalina Island was the Chaplin-Air-Line, owned by Syd Chaplin, who was a comedian and silent screen star and brother of Charlie Chaplin. Here, the plane, a Loening Amphibian, prepared to take off for Catalina on July 12, 1919, with Emery Rogers and A. C. Burns, who was the pilot. On the plane's first flight, engine trouble forced it down at sea and it had to be towed into Avalon harbor. Screen stars, including Mabel Normand, Robert Warwick, Lottie Pickford, and Kenneth Harlan, vied to go on the maiden trip. (Ronnie)

*Well, it's supposed to be a "Curtiss Seagull" and it looks like the Curtiss Seagull pic'd in AVIATION mag, Jan 1, 1920, p. 471. (see copy.)

ACTOR TOM MIX, before he became a cowboy star, sits behind the wheel of a car for the picture *The Speed Maniac* in 1919. The car is the same one he rode to victory in the Pacific Coast Amateur Championship Race at Ascot Park on July 20, 1919. (Ronnie)

[105]

THE DESCENDANTS of a Mexican era in California, led by Joe Rivera, dance in the old tradition at a Los Angeles park fiesta around 1920. The men and women, and even the small boy sitting at the feet of the musicians, dressed up in authentic old California style for the occasion. The music, too, was from an era of the old dons and the great ranchos. (Title)

THE UNIVERSITY OF SOUTHERN CALIFORNIA welcomed back its Olympic heroes from the 1920 games with a parade and cheering crowds. In this car were "Speek" George Schiller (standing left), Gwynn Wilson (standing right), and Gus A. Walker (driving). In the middle seat were, left to right, Bob McMasters, Mrs. Fred Bushmeyer, and Charles W. Paddock. Roy Evans and an unidentified woman were in the rear seat. Paddock was the only medalist, winning the gold for running the 100 meters in 10.8 seconds. Schiller competed in the 400 meters, and Evans in the discus. (USC)

THE BEVERLY HILLS SPEEDWAY had a five-year existence from 1919 to 1924 at the corner of what is now Santa Monica and Wilshire boulevards, part of the track being where the Beverly Wilshire Hotel stands today. The speedway, built entirely of lumber, was in the form of a parabola, which allowed for high speeds, and was designed in 1919 from plans by Arthur C. Pillsbury, a structural engineer. It was owned by the Beverly Hills Speedway Syndicate, which had purchased the land from the Rodeo Land and Water Company. At one point during its short life, it was totally destroyed by fire, but was quickly rebuilt. The track, which used only Triple A drivers booked by the American Automobile Association, was welcomed in the city, and attracted large crowds for its races. However, the property became so valuable, that in 1924 the track was torn down to make room for real estate subdivisions. (CSAF)

Setting New Records: 1920 to 1929

LOS ANGELES EXPLODED in every direction in every way. Records were set in real estate, office building, home building, commerce, manufacturing, shipping, shipbuilding, movie production, oil production, and in population which amazingly zoomed up from 575,000 to more than 1,200,000. Surprisingly, those who didn't want to live in Los Angeles at least wanted to visit. Tourists, led by the Crown Prince and Princess of Sweden, arrived in record numbers from all over the nation and the world.

What they saw was a continuation of the building boom. One of the top attractions was a saucer dug in the earth of Exposition Park. It was the Coliseum, a stadium built for sporting events, shows, and various exhibitions, that came to life with a football game between the University of Southern California and the University of California and attracted eighty thousand screaming fans. The visitors also gawked at the new $9-million City Hall, which was Los Angeles' tallest building, and wandered around and through its corridors that combined Greek, Roman, and American architectural styling.

Hollywood's influence reached a peak as the public grew fascinated with the film stars, and lusted for word of their love affairs, divorces, murders, and ballyhooed parties. Yet, it took an evangelist, not a movie idol, to shake the city up as it never had been before. The famous Aimee Semple McPherson mysteriously disappeared from Venice Beach, and everyone thought she had drowned while swimming. The city was in an uproar. Memorial services were held, and Los Angeles was as excited as if a President had disappeared. Later, she returned as big as life, claiming she had been kidnapped and held for ransom in a shack in the desert, but had managed to escape. It was discovered, however, that she had not been kidnapped, but had shared a cottage with a man at Carmel-by-the-Sea in Northern California. As a result, Aimee from then on was in the eyes of her public reduced to being a mere mortal. Although a bit tarnished, somewhat less than saintly, she continued with her preaching.

Los Angeles was the movie capital of the world, and proved it with *The Jazz Singer*, the first talking picture, with Al Jolson singing. Thereafter, the silents became antiques, and anyone who could speak more than two words and sound like he meant it had a chance to be in pictures.

In addition, there was more aviation activity in Los Angeles County than in any other part of the United States. California had more licensed aircraft than any other state, was number one in the nation in aircraft production, and became the first to establish daily transcontinental air service between Los Angeles and New York City. Passengers on planes operated by the Universal Aviation Corporation and Western Air Express could fly from the West Coast to the East in thirty-six hours, and had to make only one overnight stop along the way.

Not only did the black gold continue to flow, but more was discovered. A new oil field, owned by the Ohio Oil Company, was developed west of Venice. Production from its first well amounted to between twenty-five hundred and three thousand barrels a day.

Los Angeles, at this stage of its life, had everything it could ask for. About all that was left was to host an Olympiad, and that was set for 1932, with the city already deeply engrossed in making plans.

ONE OF THE GREAT CAMERAMEN of his day was William M. Blackwell of Hearst International Newsreel. Blackwell, who must have been as much a daredevil as the stuntmen he shot, on many occasions filmed Ormer Locklear's air acrobatics, including the one which killed the stuntman on August 2, 1920. Here's the primitive way Blackwell secured his tripod and camera, a Moye, to his plane, and the dangerous way he had to stand up in his open seat in order to see what he was shooting. The Curtiss Jenny belonged to the Mercury Aviation Company. (Locklear)

ORMER LOCKLEAR, the famous stuntman and silent-screen star, was given a hero's funeral, complete with soldiers and marching band, following his fatal air crash on August 3, 1920, while filming night scenes over Mercury Field for the serial *The Flywayman.* The procession was going by the Southern Pacific depot at Central and Ceres avenues when this picture was taken. (Locklear)

DeMILLE FIELD NO. 2, owned by movie producer-director Cecil B. DeMille, was located on the corner of Crescent Avenue (now Fairfax Avenue), running north and south on the right, and Wilshire Boulevard, running east and west in foreground. The billboard sign at left says, "Fly and Learn to Fly with the Mercury. Reliable Planes. Reliable Pilots. Former Army Instructors." Note the oil wells, part of the Los Angeles City Oil Field, in background, and the line up of DeMille's Mercury Aviation planes. About to land on the field in 1920 was the Goodyear "Pony" blimp. (Locklear)

GETTING A BLAST at one of the first Easter Sunrise Services ever held in the Hollywood Bowl are some of the society leaders of the early 1920s. These included Mrs. Artie Mason Carter, Mrs. Walter K. Tuller, Katherine Stone, Hugo Kirchhofer, and Charles Cadman. Mrs. Carter, as head of the Hollywood Community Chorus, inaugurated the Easter Sunrise Service at the Bowl in 1921. There were no seats available that year, and people attending the service had to find a place to sit, on the ground or on the side of the hill. (Fraggi)

THESE LOCAL LASSIES were entered in one of the most popular contests of the day, the annual Venice-Ocean Park queen contest. Although the winner probably only received a cup in 1923, there was always a chance that the queen could win fame and fortune if she could work her way into the movies. Note the old-style bathing suits and hair coverings. (H-E)

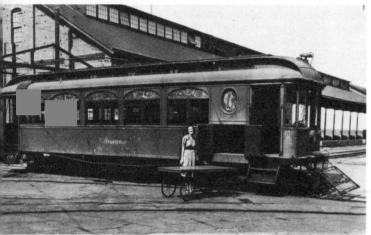

MANY A LOS ANGELES RESIDENT went to their final resting place prior to 1921 in this car, *Descanso,* and its companion trolley, *Paraiso.* The cars were made available for funerals by the Los Angeles Railway, which kept them at car barns until they were rented. The Los Angeles Railway served all cemeteries until the cars were taken out of service when it became more practical for funeral parlors to use the automobile. The casket was carried in a front compartment, accessible from the side, while mourners rode in the back. (H-E)

MRS. CLARA PHILLIPS, once referred to as California's most notorious woman killer, was on her way to San Quentin prison in 1923 under strong guard when a photographer took this picture at the railroad station in Los Angeles. The famous "Tiger Girl" was convicted of murdering, with a dime-store hammer, her best friend, Alberta Meadows, whom she thought was her husband's secret lover. She was paroled from the women's prison at Tehachapi in 1935. One of the more sensational aspects of the case was her escape from Los Angeles County jail in 1923 and, afterwards, finding her in Honduras. (H-E)

THIS BUSY THOROUGHFARE was the main street of Lankershim when it was annexed to Los Angeles in 1923. The town, which was greatly influenced by the movie industry and had many film stars and bit players within its 4,890 acres, changed its name to North Hollywood in 1927. (H-E)

THE POST-WAR BOOM that continued in Los Angeles through 1923 hit its peak by the end of the year. People had money to spend and shoppers were everywhere, as this crowd at Seventh Street and Broadway shows. It was a year of exceptional prosperity, topped off by a population jump which reached one million. Motion picture production rose to new heights, with investments in real estate, studios, and equipment totaling $750 million for approximately a hundred and fifty producers. Over 400 oil wells, capable of producing 700,000 barrels a day, were completed in the Los Angeles basin, and building valuations climbed to a strong $200 million. Also, 1,057 new tracts were put on the market, and apartments and dwellings for 40,000 families were constructed. (Ormond)

[112] EUGENE PLUMMER is shown seated on his horse on the far left. Known as the last of the Spanish dons, he supervised the killing of a steer on July 4, 1923, on his ranch in Hollywood. Only the men on horseback participated in this traditional ceremony, but everyone, including the children, usually watched the activity. Afterward, everyone would sit together in this specially decorated outdoor structure and enjoy a meal, which generally consisted of meat, beans, and salad. (Title)

THE EXPERIMENT THAT FAILED was an attempt to foster interest in horse racing in the Los Angeles area during 1923-1924. Sponsored by the Southern California Jockey Club, a betless meeting that was advertised to run for 100 days started on December 25, 1923, at Culver City Race Track, a one-mile oval. Six races were held opening day at a hastily constructed plant located south of the present MGM studio, bounded by what is now Culver and Overland boulevards, Jackson Avenue, and La Ballona Creek. Some twenty thousand persons, including society leaders, civic leaders, city officials, sportsmen, actors, athletes, and other prominent individuals attended. The winner of the first race on opening day, which this picture shows, was Orleana Girl. Tutt was second, Conichon third, and Au Revoir fourth. (H-E)

[113]

LIBRARY DIRECTORS laid the cornerstone for the new Central Public Library building located on "Norman Hill," where the old Norman School had stood for many years on May 3, 1925, before a crowd of local citizens. Directors at the special ceremonies were, left to right, Everett R. Perry, librarian; Frank Hervey Pettingell; Mrs. J. Wells Smith; and Mrs. Otto J. Zahn, kneeling with trowel. The library building was paid for with a $2.5 million bond issue passed by voters in 1921. (Shanfeld)

THE LOS ANGELES COUNTY JAIL building had been long condemned by the Los Angeles City Health Department when this view was taken in 1930. The jail, considered a veritable Bastille when it was constructed in 1902, was considered unsanitary and unfit for occupancy in its last days. Located at the corner of Justicia and Temple streets, during its peak years it held approximately 150 prisoners. It was used until 1926, when prisoners were transferred to a new Hall of Justice, which served dually as a jail and as a courthouse. (LACSD)

[114]

KEROSENE AND GASOLINE were transported in Los Angeles by horse-drawn rigs in the 1920s, long after the motor truck appeared on the local scene. In later years, however, pipelines carried the oil and eliminated the horse over the long haul. What remained from those days was the term, "tankwagon price," which is still part of oil industry language. (SPNB)

A FAMILIAR TOURIST ATTRACTION of the 1920s was Gay's Lion Farm in El Monte. Charlie Gay started the farm in 1920 and supplied lions to zoos, circuses, amusement parks, and movies. This picture shows Numa, a famous movie lion, and Mrs. Gay entertaining visitors. (Alcana)

JACK DEMPSEY, the world's heavyweight boxing champion from 1919 to 1926, was in Hollywood in 1925 starring in the movie *Manhattan Madness*. Shaking hands with James J. Corbett here, the ex-heavyweight champion (left) was on his way to Chatsworth by railroad with one hundred characters and extras for the movie. (CSAF)

THE COVINA UNION High School football team of 1926 won the Southern California Interscholastic championship. With Wallace "Chief" Newman as coach, the team defeated Inglewood High School at the Coliseum on December 18, 1926, by a 7-0 score. On the team was Gaius Shaver, who afterwards went to the University of Southern California where he became an All-American and one of the all-time great Trojan heroes. Shaver played halfback, quarterback, and fullback, and was a kicker, passer, runner, and defensive standout for USC. Covina High School also won the Southern California Interscholastic championship in 1926 and 1928. (Shanfeld)

CALISTHENICS AND EXERCISE in 1926 wasn't at all like the physical education of today and, what's more, wasn't meant to be. Yesterday's children, inhibited by their regular school clothes and their teachers, merely bent slightly from the waist in one direction, and afterwards in another. If they really wanted to create a stir, they would engage in some predetermined steps that looked more like a polite dance than physical exercise. Women's libbers should note that boys and girls weren't segregated into separate classes. Togetherness was the key. (H-E)

[116]

A VIEW OF HOLLYWOOD BOULEVARD in 1926 shows the "Big Red Cars" and Grauman's Chinese Theater (right), which was opened between Sycamore Avenue and Orange Drive that same year. Grauman, a Hollywood showman, show producer, and theater builder, also became famous for the idea of immortalizing the hand- and footprints of the stars in concrete in the lobby of his theater, and for the lavish premieres he held there. As a result, the theater grew to be one of the city's biggest tourist attractions.

THE "FOUR HORSEMEN" of Western Air Lines (Western Air Express) were the first pilots the company hired when it started flying mail from Vail Field on April 17, 1926, from Los Angeles to Salt Lake City. Standing in front of their Douglas M-2 biplane, they were (left to right) Fred Kelly, Jimmy James, Al DeGarmo, and Maury Graham. On the far right was Maj. Corliss C. Moseley, the line's first operations manager. To decide who would make the first flight, the pilots flipped coins, and James won. He took off at 7:29 a.m. (Western)

[117]

BEVERLY HILLS wanted humorist Will Rogers, the "cowboy philospher," as its mayor in 1926, and gave the famous entertainer a royal welcome when he returned from Europe after touring as Pres. Calvin Coolidge's "Ambassador of Good Will." Rogers was presented with a five-foot scroll that established him as mayor before a turn-out of movie actors, motorcycle police, two brass bands, banner and placard carriers, and residents. Almost a year later, however, Rogers' term as mayor came to an end when the city discovered that the president of the board of trustees was their legal mayor. (Title)

PRODUCER-DIRECTOR Cecil B. De-Mille directs the *King of Kings* at his DeMille Studio in 1926. The studio at 9336 Washington Boulevard in Culver City was built by Thomas Ince in 1919. After DeMille, it became Pathe Studios, Selznick, RKO, Desilu, and Paramount. (DeMille)

A VIEW OF THE UNITED ARTISTS studio owned by Mary Pickford, Douglas Fairbanks, Charlie Chaplin, and D. W. Griffith around 1926 at 7200 Santa Monica Boulevard: The studio, formed in 1919, was purchased from Benjamin B. Hampton in 1920. The set in the foreground was for the *Thief of Baghdad*, made in 1925 with Douglas Fairbanks. (Title)

BETH TOPLITZKY, daughter of Mr. and Mrs. Joe Toplitzky, celebrated her eighth birthday in a circus tent specially constructed in her parents' gardens at 415 South Windsor Boulevard in 1926. The party, one of the more elaborate social events of the year for children, featured clowns, balloons, and animals, and friends, relatives, and neighbors participated. Joe Toplitzky was a leading real estate and insurance man who utilized billboard space around the city to advertise his various businesses. (Fraggi)

THE HOLLYWOOD STUDIO CLUB provided housing, counseling, and friends to thousands of girls from its beginning in 1916 at 6129 Carlos Avenue in the heart of Hollywood. A home away from home mostly for aspiring young actresses, the club was located in this three-story stucco structure until 1926 when it moved into larger quarters. To live in the home, girls had to be between eighteen and thirty years, and could only stay for a three-year period. Many of Hollywood's most successful screen personalities lived at the club while they received their start in the business, including such luminaries as Gale Storm, Marilyn Monroe, Linda Darnell, Janet Blair, Maureen O'Sullivan, Barbara Hale, Myrna Loy, Barbara Eden, Donna Reed, Nancy Kwan, Zazu Pitts, Dolores Del Rio, Lupe Valez, and Mae Busch. (Alcana)

[119]

WITH 1164 MILES OF TRACK and approximately nine hundred rail cars, the Pacific Electric Railway was the world's most extensive electric interurban passenger system by 1926, and was a dominant factor in the pattern of population growth in Southern California. Here at the corner of Hollywood Boulevard and Highland Avenue, a traffic officer directs traffic from his box in the middle of the intersection. The streetcar, waiting for boarding passengers, also made stops in Beverly Hills, Sawetelle, the location of the National Veterans' Home, and in Venice. (PER)

ALTHOUGH LOS ANGELES gained a reputation for its bungalow style of architecture after its adobe days, almost every design popular in the world could be found in the city. For example, on its hillside in 1927 this house owned by W. C. Hay had been designed by Charles Kyson in early Italian Renaissance, characteristic of the architecture of the hill towns of Northern Italy. (Kyson)

ONE OF THE BIGGEST SOCIAL EVENTS of the 1927 season turned out to be the opening of the Hotel Flintridge in Pasadena. Fashionable social leaders, prominent businessmen, and civic leaders attended the formal dinner and dance that highlighted the opening of the $1 million hotel on December 13. The hotel, on a hill overlooking Pasadena, had one hundred rooms and ten bungalows, an outside swimming pool, and other recreational activities. Of Spanish design, one of the hotel's more lavish features was its artificial lake located in the lobby.

[121]

HIGH-RISE BUILDINGS, traffic congestion, and paved streets were a way of life in downtown Los Angeles by 1927. Here at Fifth and Main streets, one of the busiest corners in the city, stood the Title Insurance Building (right), the Citizens National Bank Building (right), the Security Building (left), and the famous Alexandria Hotel (left). (H-E)

WHEN CHUG WILSON FELL off Broken Box in 1927, he was only practicing for Los Angeles' first annual rodeo, which was held for many years at the American Legion Speedway on Alhambra Boulevard. More than two hundred performers competed that initial year in the rodeo held under the auspices of American Legion Post 27. (CSAF)

PICKWICK SYSTEMS started using a buffet coach in July 1927 on its runs between Los Angeles, El Paso, and San Diego. This observation-dining car was equipped with food and a lavatory, two items which eliminated the need for making stops. Note the upper deck for passengers, and the raised unit in front for the driver. (Bayrd)

DURING THE PROSPEROUS YEARS of the 1920s, youths were encouraged to save their pennies in small banks supplied by the Twenty-Fifth Street and Central Avenue branch of the Merchants' National Trust and Savings Bank. Not only were the children given banks, but as part of the bank's promotion, they were also supplied with "Thrift" hats. Here at the bank in 1927, youngsters from the Staunton Avenue Elementary School line up to deposit their weekly savings. (H-E)

A FAVORITE ABOLONE FISHING SPOT in the early 1900s was this fisherman station at White Point on the Palos Verdes Peninsula. In those days, fishing for abalone was a favorite pastime of the Chinese and Japanese, who found their abalone along the rocks and crevices, or just off shore in shallow water. (Title)

GIRLS CALLED ATTENTION to just about anything and everything in Los Angeles, and sometimes even managed to get into the newspapers. This ballet dancer in 1927 was used to show off the efficiency trophy presented by Los Angeles insurance men to fire chief Ralph J. Scott. The trophy was awarded for Los Angeles' low loss per capita from fire during the years 1921-1926. But was the chief too shy to hold his own trophy? (LAFD)

A HUGE CROWD of 80,000 persons, many of them school children, greeted Charles Lindbergh (left) in Los Angeles Memorial Coliseum on September 20, 1927. Lindbergh shook hands with Joe Scott, gave a speech, and that evening attended a banquet in his honor at the Ambassador Hotel. Lindbergh was on the last leg of a national tour to promote public interest in aviation, following his solo, non-stop transatlantic flight from New York City to Paris, France, on May 21, 1927. When he landed in Los Angeles at Vail Field in his *Spirit of St. Louis,* he was greeted by 150,000 people and then paraded through the city's business district on his way to the Coliseum. The next day he flew to San Diego. (CSAF)

[123]

THE ARMY took over in the beginning 1920s to highlight a celebration marking the end of World War I. While this drill team and band entertained the Redondo Beach citizens, the Pacific Electric Railway continued picking up and dropping off passengers in the background. The "Big Red Cars" started their runs to Redondo in 1891, and in the early 1900s carried people on excursions to the city to see its large hotel, busy wharf, and fields of colorful carnations. (Title)

YOUTHS OF AN ORPHANS' HOME on El Centro Avenue in Hollywood swarm over Los Angeles Fire Department vehicles in 1927 to receive their jars of jam. Three tons of such sweets, collected by Fire Department members, were contributed annually to orphans' homes in the Los Angeles area. (LAFD)

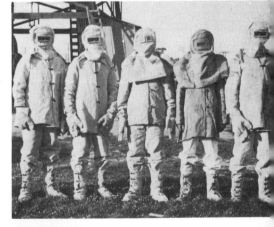

THESE WEREN'T MEN FROM MARS, but only an "asbestos crew" from the Union Oil Company. The oil firm started battling fires at its Southern California oil fields with such crews in 1927. The suits, which enabled the men to actually walk through flames, protected them from the intense heat also. (H-E)

HOLLYWOOD'S FIRST CITIZENS returned for an "old settlers picnic" in 1927 at Plummer Park. They were, left to right, Robert Young, first city attorney; Sanford Rich, first mayor; E. Fossler, first chief of the colunteer firemen; G. T. Gower, first town marshal; G. G. Greenwood, first banker; Mrs. Ben Moeller, first librarian; and Mrs. Mamie Sackett, first postmistress. (H-E)

THE LOS ANGELES TUBERCULOSIS ASSOCIATION maintained a children's health camp high in the Sierra Madre Mountains in San Gabriel Canyon in 1927. More than one hundred boys who suffered from the disease enjoyed the fresh air and sunshine, and daily performed exercises in an attempt to build up their undernourished bodies. The camp was supported through funds raised from the sale of Tuberculosis Christmas Seals. (H-E)

JESSE HIBBS, who later became a film director, in 1928 showed the form that made him an All-American tackle and backfield man for the University of Southern California. Hibbs was mainly a director of "B" features in Hollywood from 1953 to 1958, and directed nine movies. His first was *All American* in 1953. (H-E)

CHINESE CHILDREN in their colorful Oriental dress pull a cart that was used in a special benefit Chinatown show that was held in downtown Los Angeles in 1927. The show, in which the children appeared, was part of the Chinese community's New Year's celebration, which called for prayers, much feasting, and singing. (Danning)

TO BE THE FIRST to transport a live animal by air across a continent, Metro-Goldwyn-Mayer studio in 1927 put its famous Leo the Lion in a Ryan B.I. monoplane, with Martin Jensen as pilot, and watched them take off from San Diego for New York City. Leo, in a specially constructed steel cage surrounded by a glass shield to keep out the wind, was located directly behind the pilot. Trapped in a canyon while flying over Arizona, Jensen crashed into the rugged Mongollon Mountains, but he was unhurt when he wandered from the mountains three days later, as was Leo, who continued on his way by truck.

BILLIE COPELAND of Los Angeles was the California entry in the Atlantic City Miss America beauty pageant in 1927. She didn't win. However, in 1935 she married Earl Lambeau, who was then the famous coach of the Green Bay Packers of the national professional football league.

[127]

MARATHON DANCING reached its peak in Los Angeles around 1928 when it was banned by the Los Angeles City Council because it was dangerous to the health of the participants. Dancers suffered blistered feet, aching muscles, cramps, and other ills, and on many occasions had to be taken by ambulance to hospitals for treatment. Some marathon dancers continued their movements for as long as 260 hours, and wore out orchestras, forcing dance floor managers to use phonographic music as substitutes.

This picture taken in 1928 shows the finalists in a marathon dancing contest held at the Bon Ton Ballroom in Ocean Park. Soon after this dance, it became a misdemeanor to participate in dances, runs, rolls, walks, crawls, or in any other endurance contests, and persons caught were subject to a $500 fine or six months in jail, or both. (H-E)

WOMEN'S LIBBERS fighting for equal rights in sports can point with pride to the first female football team in Southern California, the "Baby Tigers," at Occidental College in 1928. Football may have been a bit rough for the girls, but not any rougher than hockey, polo, or steeplechasing, which the ladies already had taken up in those days. Standing, left to right, were Jane Ryden, Anita Simonson, Bonnie Lamp, Dot Burch, and Capt. Alice Ryden. Kneeling, left to right, were Miss Brininstool, Ludy Buell, Lois Ellenberger, Mary Crawford, Marinella Wimp, and Lou Stadlinger. (H-E)

DR. JOHN J. Seiler, the "Flying Yank," ran all the way from San Diego to Los Angeles with a letter of greetings from Mayor Harry Clark to Mayor George E. Cryer in 1928. He completed the 150-mile, non-stop run in twenty-four hours. Dr. Seiler had gained fame and the title of the "Flying Yank" in 1927 when he ran from Atlantic City, New Jersey, to Los Angeles in 57 days. (H-E)

MEMBERS OF THE PASADENA GIRLS CLUB practice their starts in March 1928 in preparation for the Olympic trials later in the year. They are, left to right, Nellie Doerschlay, Rayma Wilson, Anna Urana, Ruth Webster, and Ethel Nichols. The Olympics were opened to women for the first time in 1928. (H-E)

DIRECTOR LEO Le BLANC tried to set a serious mood while training his girls on the roof of a Los Angeles skyscraper for the opening of a new show, *Sally,* in 1928. Le Blanc claimed that the best way to chase the kinks out of calves was to expose them to Los Angeles' bright sunshine. The girls in the cast, of course, are hanging on to his every word—or are they? (H-E)

THIS FENCING TEAM representing the Los Angeles Athletic Club competed against San Francisco in 1928 for the Pacific Coast Championships at the club in downtown Los Angeles. Members were (left to right, bottom row) Leonard Beckham, A. R. Jaquith, and James Reed, Jr., and (left to right, top row) H. J. Uyttenhove, J. L. Thompson, C. D. Cathcart, John Duff, and H. C. Berls. (H-E)

PUPILS OF THE VERNON CITY SCHOOL, which was in a district annexed to Los Angeles in 1928, posed in front of their bungalows that same year. Constructed in 1896, the bungalows were small, dark, and generally inadequate, and were scheduled to be torn down if voters in 1928 approved a $29 million school bond issue. The issue was passed and a new school replaced the bungalows. (LAUSD)

ELABORATE FLOATS carrying costumed participants, marching bands, horse units, and automobiles filled with civic leaders, took part in a parade in honor of the new Los Angeles City Hall. The City Hall, a stately pyramid-type building which cost $5 million, was dedicated and opened on April 26, 1928. One of the parade's most original floats *(below)*, was sponsored by the Chinese Consolidated Benevolent Association. (Danning)

A NEW UNIT of the Roosevelt Highway, which stretched from Canada to Mexico along the Pacific Coast, opened in 1929 between Santa Monica and Oxnard. For the first time cars were able to travel along the coast on the famous Malibu ranch property, which was one of the original Spanish land grants. (H-E)

THE FLAG-DRAPED COFFIN carrying the body of the late Sen. Frank Putnam Flint was carried by pallbearers down the Los Angeles City Hall steps following funeral services on February 16, 1929. Senator Flint's body, which lay in state guarded by eight marines, was taken to Glendale's Forest Lawn Memorial Park, where he was buried in private services. Flint served as a senator from 1905 to 1911, and was known for guaranteeing an unlimited water supply for Southern California from the Colorado River. Also, Senator Flint at one time led a fight to station warships in the Pacific Ocean, and to have a fleet based at Los Angeles Harbor. (H-E)

PILOT ART GOEBEL (left) was greeted by 75,000 cheering onlookers at Mines Field when he landed in Los Angeles in 1928 in this Lockheed Vega called the *Yankee Doodle*. Goebel flew nonstop from New York City to break the transcontinental record in 18 hours and 58 minutes. With Goebel in Los Angeles, prior to his historic flight, was Allen Loughhead, the plane's designer. The *Yankee Doodle* was owned by Harry Tucker, a pilot and wealthy Santa Monica flying enthusiast. (Danning)

[132]

WHILE ON A FLIGHT from San Diego to San Francisco, this squadron of Army planes flew over Grand Central Air Terminal, Glendale, at airport dedication ceremonies on February 22, 1929, as 30,000 spectators looked on. The field, one of the largest in the world when it opened, was known for the movies made there, for parties held in the terminal bar by movie stars who saw friends off to New York and Mexico City, for actor Wallace Beery and his air stunts, and for the famous people who landed and took off from the airport during the thirty years of its existence. the airport was closed on July16, 1959, when it gave way to industrial development. (Title)

EVANGELIST AIMEE SEMPLE McPHERSON, one of the most talked about figures in Los Angeles history in 1929, waved goodbye to a small group of admirers at Union Station before she boarded a train for Sacramento, where she was to testify at an impeachment trial. Her two children, Roberta (left) and Rolf (right), accompanied her to the station, but did not go along on the trip. (H-E)

WHEN THE LAST UNIT of the Roosevelt Highway was opened in 1929, Miss Canada (left), Miss Phyllis Petit of Oxnard, and Miss Mexico, Miss Margaret Watt of Santa Monica, were on hand for the special ceremonies. (H-E)

THE NATION'S FIRST ALL-METAL DIRIGIBLE, the *City of Glendale*, left its hangar at Grand Central Air Terminal, Glendale, for a test flight in 1929, but was ripped by an explosion soon after this picture was taken. Engineers for the Slate Aircraft Company, builders of the dirigible, claimed the sun had built up a super pressure inside the gas container, and caused the riveting to give way. The ship was expected to fly at a speed of 100 mph., and was to carry forty passengers. (H-E)

[133]

THE FIRST CONSTRUCTION for the University of California at Los Angeles campus in Westwood was the steps which led to the gymnasium in 1929. At that time, UCLA was considered "way out" from Los Angeles, and was surrounded by open fields and hills. Sunset Boulevard, which stretched from Beverly Hills through the hills past the campus out toward the ocean, was on the right. (CSAF)

THE THIMBLE CLUB of the Glendale Women's Auxiliary, Spanish-American War veterans, repaired an American flag found by Frank Lawrence, Glendale commander, when he fought in the Philippines. This flag-sewing activity took place in 1929 at a Betsy Ross party at the home of Mrs. Catherine Litspreu in Glendale. (Alcana)

THIS "BROKEN BLOSSOM," as the Los Angeles police called her, was a drug addict who surfaced in Los Angeles after being cast out of Chinatown in 1929. She was the daughter of a wealthy Pasadena family, and had given up home, friends, family, and a possible career to live for many years as a slave with the Chinese, who kept her in line by supplying her with drugs. (H-E)

[134]

THE ADMIRAL LINER *Dorothy Alexander* was a familiar sight to Los Angeles' coastal population around 1929 when the ship became the first to cruise between Los Angeles and Alaska. Constructed in 1907 as *The President* for the Pacific Coast Company, the 417-foot long vessel carried a total 225 passengers and could sail at 17 knots. The ship set another first during its initial year of existence when in 1907, 300 miles from Nome, Alaska, it became the first ship on the North Pacific Coast to broadcast a commercial radio message.

AT THE COIN TOSS for the 1929 Rose Bowl game between Georgia Tech and California were (left to right) Peter Pund, Georgia Tech's All-American center and captain; referee Herb Dana; and Irv Phillips, California's captain. The game that year attracted 71,000 persons, who paid $270,000 to see Georgia Tech win 8-7. Also, it was the year that California center, Roy Riegels, recovered a Georgia fumble and ran the wrong way. (CSAF)

AFTER A TWO-YEAR LAYOFF, girls field hockey was revived at the University of Southern California in 1929. One of the most popular of the coed sports, field hockey was played much in the manner of ice hockey, with the ball hit or passed from player to player upfield to a net, where the goals were scored. Participants were, left to right, Margaret Rendzik, Leonora Rathburn, Mary Plesko, and Helen Pechke. (USC)

[135]

LAVISH MANSIONS owned by wealthy citizens and movie stars dotted the Hollywood Hills in 1930. The sign "Hollywoodland" (right), almost on top of the mountain, was 75 feet high, about 450 feet long, and was located on Los Angeles-owned property in what is now Griffith Park. It was originally put up for a real estate development, but became so well known and popular over the years since its construction in 1923 that the "land" was dropped, and the "Hollywood" remained as a historic-cultural monument.

[136]   THIS PICTURE of the Los Angeles Harbor in San Pedro, taken in 1930, shows the Los Angeles Shipbuilding and Dry Dock Company, right, and its launching ramps to its left. Above the shipbuilding firm is the Standard Oil tank farm, and next to it, the old Pacific Electric Railway drawbridge. On the other side (left) of the bridge are the American Mail and American President Lines terminals, and behind them in the background is Brighton Beach. In foreground is a dry dock, which is still there at the same location. The Los Angeles Shipbuilding and Dry Dock Comapny, which still exists, was organized in 1917, and immediately received $70 million in contracts for the construction of steel ships. (Spence)

Hit by a Depression: 1930 to 1939

ALONG WITH THE REST of the nation, Los Angeles was hit hard by the Depression. Some four hundred thousand persons walked the streets, without money for food or rent. Countless real estate investors found themselves with taxes to pay, and with little or no income. It was a time of despair. Thousands, in order to support themselves, discovered the Works Progress Administration, and were engaged at parks and playgrounds, in the improvement of school buildings, in art projects, in music, in the theater, in historical research, or in writing. And as Angelenos fought merely to survive, other people, even more impoverished, looked toward the city as the Promised Land.

In sports, the tenth Olympiad stuck out like a sore thumb during a decade that saw the Depression put a stranglehold on the nation. The Coliseum was enlarged to seat 105,000 persons, and, in the midst of all the adversity, was turned into the biggest stadium in the world. For the first time, an Olympic village was constructed. Consisting of 600 bungalows, it was located in the Baldwin Hills and housed the forty competing nations' 1,300 male athletes, trainers, coaches, and chefs who could look out over the city and the oil-derricked hills.

In the mid-1930s, migrants came from the Dust Bowl, as many as three hundred and fifty thousand streaming in from Oklahoma, Texas, Arkansas, Missouri, and Kansas. Everyone had heard of Los Angeles. It was a paradise, a land of milk and honey and oranges, where one could make a completely new start. They pushed their way west without money, and Los Angeles, mercilessly, tried to stop them. A special army of Los Angeles police was stationed at the California-Nevada border to check trains for them and to halt the Los-Angeles-bound hitchhikers. The action was ludicrous and desperate, however, and lasted only two months.

Making matters worse, Long Beach and Compton and the area south of Los Angeles were struck by an earthquake in which 120 people lost their lives. Buildings tumbled, land cracked, and homes were destroyed. It was as if God had sent down a warning to the Southern Californians.

[137]

In any case, disillusioned with the economic system, Angelenos in droves sought something better. Out of this atmosphere appeared *Technocracy* and the *Utopian Society* and a Dr. Francis E. Townsend, who advocated that the federal government give $200 a month to everyone over sixty years old, with the requirement that the entire allowance be spent each month to stimulate the economy. Townsend was hailed as a deliverer, and his movement became as zealous as a religious crusade. Yet like many other schemes arising out of bad times, the movement came to a halt when it was discovered that Townsend had milked his collections, donated by the elderly, of almost $80,000 for personal use. This and the subsequent start of the Social Security System, led to his decline.

Next came another migration to swell the city's already-bursting seams, with national defense playing the role of economic savior, and Pres. Franklin D. Roosevelt as its disciple. Near the close of the decade, Roosevelt ordered the construction of 10,000 airplanes in order to fight a war he envisioned in the nation's future. Thus, thousands of people rushed pell-mell across the continent to work in the huge, sprawling, new factories. Once again, Angelenos had money jingling in their pockets, roofs over their heads, and a chicken in every pot. Who said Los Angeles wasn't the Promised Land?

EDWARD L. DOHENY struck oil on this spot in 1892, and started the Los Angeles gold fever with a frenzy. The rig was located off Glendale Boulevard, between Colton and Patton streets, not far from the downtown Plaza area. Doheny was the one who found the drill site, and with his partner, Charles A. Canfield, paid $400 for the lot. This picture shows Doheny, in a white straw hat, waving to the crowd, on the rig in 1930 when he returned to the scene for a dedication ceremony. (Fraggi)

THOUSANDS LINED THE RUNWAY and visited the hangars and new operations building for the dedication of the Los Angeles Municipal Airport in 1930 at Sepulveda and Century boulevards, where it still exists today. The airport originally was started in 1927, when Judge Frank D. Parent of Inglewood and a group of Los Angeles citizens chose 640 acres on the Andrew G. Bennett Rancho for the airport. In 1928, the terminal, then known as Mines Field, with no buildings and only a dirt strip for a runway, began operations. (Title)

PATRONESSES who presided at the banquet tables in the Sala de Oro at the Biltmore Hotel in 1930 helped raise money for the construction of a women's residence hall at the University of Southern California. They were, front row, Mms. Seeley W. Mudd, Rufus von Kleinsmid, Frederick W. Klamp, Henry M. Willis, Chester Wallace Brown, and Nicholas Rice. Middle row were Mmes. Charles E. Seaman, Owen H. Churchill, Wildon H. Carr, Oscar Trippet, Gurdon Wallace Wattles, and Paul H. Helms. Back row were Mmes. Thomas W. Kester, Alexander B. Barret, J. C. Early, John T. Dodge, Queen W. Boardman, A. E. D. Carscallen, E. W. Clark, William A. Moses, and Miss Ida Lindley. (USC)

STUDYING THE TORAH was one of the activities of these old scholars at the Hebrew Sheltering Home For the Aged in 1930 during the Passover holidays. Passover, the "Festival of the Unleavened Bread," as it is called in the Torah, commemorates the deliverance of the children of Israel from over two centuries of Egyptian bondage, and recalls their mass exodus from Egypt about 3,300 years ago. (Alcana)

THE WILLIAM FOX STUDIO was constructed on this site on Western Avenue and Sunset Boulevard in 1915 by Thomas Dixon, author of the movie *The Klansman*. In 1917, Dixon sold the studio to William Fox, who rebuilt it a year later after it burned down. The studio, located on two lots intersected by Western, was owned by Fox until the 1960s, when it was sold to make way for a shopping center. Actress Theda Bara made some of her most famous movies there, as did cowboy stars Tom Mix and Buck Jones. (Title)

[140]

AFTER THE UNUSUAL and somewhat strange looking Sante Fe station opened on July 29, 1893, in the middle of a national financial crisis, it became known throughout the world by millions of persons during the forty years it stood on the corner of Sante Fe Avenue and First Street. First it was called "La Grande," and afterwards affectionately as the "Old Sante Fe Depot." When this picture was taken in the early 1930s, it had changed very little from its inception. It was of Moorish design, featured an inside trim of Oregon pine and California redwood, had separate lunch rooms for men and women, and cost approximately $50,000. Drinking fountains actually ran ice water, and in each waiting room, carved in Flagstaff sandstone, was the motto, "East or West, Sante Fe Is Best." (SFR)

PATIENTS of Duarte's Los Angeles Sanitarium, which became the City of Hope in 1946, led a quiet existence in the 1930s. Here they relaxed in beach chairs and played chess or checkers outdoors in front of the Cleveland cottage, which was the newest building on the grounds. In those days, the sanitarium, which started in 1913, handled only tubercular patients. Today the facility researches every major disease.

FERGUSON ALLEY, which ran east of the Plaza and across Alameda to Vignes Street, was the heart of Los Angeles' Chinatown in the early 1900s. Both sides of the alley were jammed with shops and homes. When the area was demolished in the 1930s to make way for Los Angeles' Union Station, tunnels were found that connected the entire Chinese community. Because of local prejudice against the Chinese, they built the passageways as a place of refuge. In these tunnels, however, were also their opium dens, gambling rooms, and even their burial pits. (LACSD)

A SEA OF UMBRELLAS was a common sight on hot days in the Southland around the 1930s. This scene south of the Long Beach Pike, which featured a roller coaster, a midway, and other rides, was typical of the Southland's hot days when huge crowds flocked to the ocean to cool off. Note that there were as many men in suits, hats, shirts, and ties as there were in bathing suits, and as many women and children who were dressed in everyday clothes as were in bathing suits. (H-E)

THE NEW CITY HALL towered over the Los Angeles County Courthouse when this picture was taken around 1930. As late as 1904, the courthouse was the chief showplace of the city, and rose majestically on Poundcake Hill, where Los Angeles High School once stood. Known for its red sandstone walls, the courthouse was one of the finest examples of Romanesque architecture in the country when it was built in 1888 (according to *Kidder's Handbook of Architecture and Building*). The five-story building was condemned in 1933, and torn down in 1938. Note the bronze statue of Sen. Stephen M. White in front of the north entrance. (Shanfeld)

THE FIRST LOCOMOTIVE to ever enter Los Angeles returned in 1931, on a truck drawn by thirty-two white horses instead of under its own power. The locomotive was part of the "Epic of Transportation" parade held during the La Fiesta celebration. Thousands of persons lining the sidewalks cheered as transportation in use through 150 years of Los Angeles history passed in review. (H-F)

GOLF ROULETTE was quick to appear and quick to fade out at the city's miniature golf courses in 1931. Players putted toward the roulette wheel, and then watched as the ball went rolling round and round until it fell into a hole. Points were scored on the basis of the number and the color of the hole. (H-E)

JAPAN'S FINE ART of ancient swordsmanship arrived in Los Angeles in 1931 when the famous master, Shusui Ansai, brought his skills to the Japanese colony. An ancient and honorable sport and form of protection, swordsmanship for these Japanese youngsters was more popular than any of the Western sports. Although the swords had no points, the youths were well protected with face masks, chest and waist guards, and heavy gloves.

WHEN SNOW FELL in Los Angeles in 1931, the city went into a state of shock. Although many people retreated indoors, youngsters had a fine time throwing snowballs and making snowmen. Unfortunately, for those who enjoyed the change in the weather, it didn't last long. The next day the snow melted. (H-E)

SCREEN COMEDIAN HAROLD LLOYD *(left)* was the Grand Marshall of the "Pageant of the Jewels," an electrical parade sponsored by the motion picture industry as part of its contribution to Los Angeles' 1931 La Fiesta celebration. Held in Los Angeles Memorial Coliseum before thousands of spectators, the parade was billed as a "million dollar turnout," and was highlighted by movie stars, beautiful girls, music, special lighting effects, and brightly decorated floats. One of the more spectacular of the floats, "Debutantes," was offered by Fox Films. On it, left to right, were Conchita Montenegro, Helen Mack, and Linda Watkins. (H-E)

PAULINE STOCKTON, who was famous as a physical fitness instructor and as a woman athletic trainer, helped keep Los Angeles women in good shape in 1931. Here she is drilling her students for their first Los Angeles public exhibition. Miss Stockton had more than 1,000 young Southern California feminine athletes enrolled in her classes. (H-E)

[144]

MILDRED GATES established telephone service between the United States and Hawaii for the first time when she plugged in the Los Angeles-Honolulu call over radio telephone at the switchboard in Pacific Telephone Company offices at 443 South Olive Street on December 23, 1931. The call was part of opening ceremonies made by government and business officials simultaneously in fourteen United States' cities, covering 100,000 miles in 30 minutes. Cost of the call between the West Coast and Honolulu was $21 for the first three minutes, and $7 for each additional minute. (PT)

SEDERS WERE HELD throughout the city as Los Angeles Jewish population celebrated Passover in 1931. This picture shows a simulated family seder at the Hebrew Sheltering Home For the Aged. Fanny Silverstein (right) was 104 years old at the time. On the table were the ingredients of the seder—wine matzah, parsley, bitter herbs, haroses, salt water, one roasted shank bone, one egg roasted or boiled, and one large wine glass or cup for the prophet Elijah.

MAYOR JOHN C. PORTER cut the ribbon that opened Spring Street from Temple Street to Sunset Boulevard. With Mayor Porter in 1932 was Senorita Consuelo Bonzo and Spanish singers and musicians, who participated with civic officials in the celebration. The new street in the early days of Los Angeles was an old cattle trail that ran around the base of Fort Moore.

MAJ. CORLISS C. MOSELEY set a record in reverse in 1931 when he established the slowest speed thought possible for an airplane. He flew 25 mph in a Curtiss Wright Junior, a pusher type aircraft that was more like a powered glider with an engine (a 3-cylinder Szekley with 45 hp). Moseley, a USC fullback and a World War I pursuit pilot, won the first Pulitzer prize race in 1920 on Long Island, New York, with a speed of 176 mph. At one time Moseley established the largest flying school in the country, was a United States Air Corps test pilot in 1929, helped start Western Air Lines, became genera? manager of Grand Central Air Terminal, and was West Coast manager of the Curtiss Wright Corporation from 1929 to 1934. (H-E)

MORE THAN 50,000 SPECTATORS gathered on July 29, 1932, for the dedication of the new State Office Building, bounded by Broadway, Court, Spring, and First streets, in downtown Los Angeles. The crowd was so dense, spilling over on lawns, Spring Street, intersections, the roof of City Hall, and other buildings in the Civic Center, that traffic was jammed for several blocks away from the dedication. The ceremony, attended by United States' Vice President Charles Curtis and California Governor James Rolph, Jr., also honored Amelia Earhart, who received the Distinguished Flying Cross for twice successfully flying across the Atlantic Ocean. The $6-million building, twelve stories high, was for judicial and administrative officials in the southern part of the state. (H-E)

IT WAS HARD for anyone in downtown Los Angeles to ignore the coming of the tenth Olympic Games in 1932. Everywhere flags of competing nations mixed with American flags, flying from department stores, hotels, and office buildings. Not only did the flags wave downtown, but also on streets leading from Los Angeles railroad stations. This was the view looking north on Broadway from Seventh Street, with Bullock's Department Store on the left. (H-E)

ITALIAN CYCLIST Attilio Pavesi was greeted by a large, cheering crowd at the finish of the Olympic Games' 100-kilometer road race in 1932. Pavesi traveled from Moorpark to Castellamare, 62.14 miles, on the California state highway in 2 hours, 28 minutes, and 5.6 seconds. Each rider in the race was escorted over the distance by a state highway patrolman. (H-E)

FRANK WYKOFF, a University of Southern California sprinter, crosses the finish line to bring victory to the Americans in the 400-meters relay event in the 1932 Olympic Games in Los Angeles. Wykoff's strong finish enabled the American team to win the event in the world-record time of 3 minutes, 8.2 seconds. (H-E)

A LOS ANGELES GIRL, Lillian Copeland, set a new woman's world record in the discus while competing for the American team in the 1932 Olympic Games at the Los Angeles Memorial Coliseum. Miss Copeland threw the discus 133 feet, 13/4 inches to beat out Ruth Osburn of Shelbyville, Missouri, who had previously held the record, for the gold medal. (H-E)

[148]

GRECIAN DANCES as they were performed in the art festival of the ancient Olympic Games were revived at the Hollywood Bowl in 1932 when the Ernest Belcher dancers presented an Olympiad ballet, with gymnasts, weight lifters, and wrestlers from the Los Angeles Athletic Club portraying ancient athletes. The program was the Hollywood Bowl's contribution to the Olympic Games.

MILDRED "BABE" DIDRIKSON, one of the greatest of women athletes, is first over the women's 80-meter hurdles, which she won in the world-record time of 11.7 seconds at the 1932 Olympic Games in Los Angeles. Babe also won the women's javelin throw, setting another world record, with a toss of 143 feet, 4 inches. She also took second in the high jump. (H-E)

GOING OVER THE HIGH JUMP BAR for a world's record at the 1932 Olympic Games in Los Angeles Memorial Coliseum was America's Jean Shiley. Miss Shiley won the event with a leap of 5 feet, 5½ inches. This event was actually won by "Babe" Didrikson, who was placed second when her "dive roll" technique was judged illegal. (H-E)

BONUS ARMY MEMBERS left Los Angeles in June 1932 for a 3,000-mile journey to Washington, D.C., where they joined thousands of other World War I veterans also demanding their bonuses. The bonus was the compensation voted by Congress for men who were in the services, up to and including the rank of captain. The bonus amounted to $1 for every day of war served after the first 60 days, and $1.25 for every day of war served overseas after the first 60 days. Hundreds of autos left Los Angeles in a caravan, and were cheered by thousands of spectators wishing them good luck. (H-E)

THE FIRST PATROL STATION opened by the Los Angeles County Sheriff's Department was this one west of Central Avenue and south of Slauson Boulevard in the Florence district. Known as the Sheriff's Office, Substation No. 1, Criminal Division, it was opened in 1924 to serve Los Angeles' growing south-central population. On November 3, 1932, local officers with their Buick patrol cars posed with motorcycle deputies, who were phased out when the State Highway Patrol took over traffic enforcement. (LACSD)

EUGENE W. BISCAILUZ was sworn in as Los Angeles County sheriff in December 1932 after he was appointed to fill the unexpired term of William I. Traeger, who had been elected to the U.S. Senate. Biscailuz, one of the most popular of the Los Angeles County sheriffs, retired in 1958, after twenty-six year's service in the position. He was succeeded by Peter J. Pitchess. Sworn in with Biscailuz (center) was Capt. Arthur Jewell, who became undersheriff.

LOS ANGELES MAYOR FRANK L. SHAW sat astride the Breakfast Club's famous wooden horse when he was initiated into the organization in 1933. Those attending the ceremony were (left to right), Harry Baine, a Los Angeles County supervisor; Orra E. Monnette, a banker who presented Shaw with his gold membership card; Shaw; Roger Jessup, a Los Angeles County supervisor; and George E. Morehand, a club director.

BATTLING AGAINST HIGHER TAXES, representatives of the property owner's division of the Los Angeles County Realty Boards massed before the Los Angeles County Board of Supervisors and demanded that the 88-cent tax rate be retained, or decreased—instead of increased. At this meeting in 1933, Harold H. Byron, then chairman of the property owner's division of the Pasadena Realty Board, stood on a chair so he could be seen by everyone, and argued against the suggested tax increase. (H-E)

A STRONG EARTHQUAKE hit the Los Angeles area in 1933. It lasted initially 22 seconds, and was followed by 150 shocks that night and the next day. The center of the quake was in Long Beach which suffered millions of dollars worth of damages. Los Angeles and Compton were also heavily affected by the tremor which destroyed 2,100 houses, damaged 21,000, and cost many lives. A man and a woman were killed by falling debris at Third Street and Pine Avenue in Long Beach *(above),* where mostly older small buildings caved in or had their sides torn away. None of the taller, modern structures were damaged. Immediately after the earthquake, the Army, Navy, and the Salvation Army set up emergency kitchens, relief stations, and distributed clothes to the homeless. To keep order, Navy personnel *(left)* patroled Long Beach streets, and the California Highway Patrol *(below)* kept out sightseers. Only those who lived in Long Beach or had official passes were allowed past this check point at Long Beach Boulevard and San Antonio Drive. (H-E)

COMPTON SUFFERED almost as much as Long Beach when the 1933 earthquake struck. After the main trembler hit, building walls shook loose and dropped on people and automobiles. As soon as the initial shock wore off, the police started searching through the debris for dead and injured, and eventually found several dead persons in this area. (H-E)

AFTER HUNTINGTON PARK Mayor Richard Scholz ordered the churches closed, following the big 1933 quake that hit some Southland coastal areas, open-air services were held in parks throughout the city. Prayer meetings such as this, conducted by the Rev. S. S. Sampson, were typical of the sessions held in this fashion until the city's building inspectors could declare the churches safe. (H-E)

THE "ALWAYS OPEN" MECCA CAFE in downtown
Long Beach lived up to its promise, despite the earthquake of 1933. Cafe employes fed people from tables
placed along the sidewalk until repairs to the building
were completed. Customers, however, had to eat where
they could, and sat on boxes or stood on the sidewalk
or in the street. For five cents you could get either
coffee, a ham sandwich, buttermilk, or two doughnuts.
(H-E)

AIMEE SEMPLE McPHERSON was a young Canadian
girl who arrived in the 1920s in Los Angeles with $100,
a tambourine, and a touring car painted with the sign,
"Jesus Is Coming Soon—Get Ready." By 1926, the
evangelist was the most vibrant and the most talked-
about personality in Southern California. This picture
shows her in 1933 when she wore her new, white uniform for the first time at Christmas day services at
Angelus Temple. A silver cross was embroidered on
the front of her gown, and about her shoulders was a
black stole. Her Bible was bound in white leather.

MEMBERS OF SERA, the State Emergency Relief Adminstration, posed for this picture prior to the first of its series of weekly radio concerts over KFAC, the official broadcasting station of *The Evening Herald and Express*. Assisting the orchestra in 1934 was a choral unit, which also was created under SERA. The orchestra contained some of the finest musicians in Southern California, and broadcast every Wednesday evening. (H-E)

ONE OF THE HEAVIEST RAIN STORMS in Southern California history hit on New Year's Eve and formed rivers of mud and water in 1934 that swept before it many homes and automobiles. This scene in the La Crescenta-Montrose section of the foothills was typical of the damage, which included the loss of lives. Muddy torrents moved this house hundreds of feet from its foundation, and buried this car so badly that there was nothing left to salvage. (H-E)

THE LOS ANGELES COUNTY FAIR at Pomona drew record breaking crowds to its midway in 1934 when people tried to forget the Great Depression. Thousands of persons enjoyed the games, rides, side shows, merry-go-round, and exhibits; and flocked to the grandstand (background) for various entertainments and the horse races. (LACF)

OFFICER ARTHUR O. BOYD demonstrates Pasadena's new radio for motorcycle policemen in 1934. The city, after a two-year experiment, was the first in the West to equip its motorcycles with short wave radios. Featuring a single control, the set fastened to the rear of the motorcycle, and the loud speaker was located on the handlebars. (H-E)

THE "SPORT OF KINGS" lured to Santa Anita Race Track in Arcadia one of its founders, Dwight Hart, for the opening of the 1934 season. With Hart in the Turf Club section reserved for founders were Dwight Hart, Jr., and Mrs. Dwight Hart. That racing season was particularly notable, because of the great number of society persons who turned out for the races. (SART)

MRS. ALPHONZO E. BELL posed in the terraced garden of her lavish mansion, Capo di Monte, in 1934. The home was used, after this picture was taken, for a local garden club show, at which rare flowers, exotic fruits, and vegetables were displayed. Mrs. Bell was the wife of Alphonzo E. Bell, a financier, an oil magnate, a real estate developer, and the sub-divider of Bel-Air, a community which was named by Mrs. Bell. (H-E)

A ROUSING OVATION was given former Pres. Herbert Hoover when he was seen by 35,000 fans who showed up in the rain at the 1934 Tournament of Roses football game in Pasadena. Coach Lou Little's Columbia eleven beat Stanford's "vow boys" 7-0. Standing next to the ex-president was Adm. William S. Sims (left). The ladies, left to right, were Mrs. Sims, Mrs. George Parker, and Mrs. Hoover. Forty-eight hours before the game, a rain storm flooded the Los Angeles area and left twelve inches of water on the field. It was still raining at the time of the game. (H-E)

VETERANS OF THE CIVIL WAR, the Spanish-American War, and World War I, in addition to the National Guard and Reserve Officer Training Corps units, marched in a Memorial Day parade at Los Angeles Memorial Coliseum in 1934. Leading the parade were the remaining members of the Grand Army of the Republic, an organization established by Civil War veterans of the Union Army and Navy. It was the G.A.R. that secured Memorial Day as a national holiday.

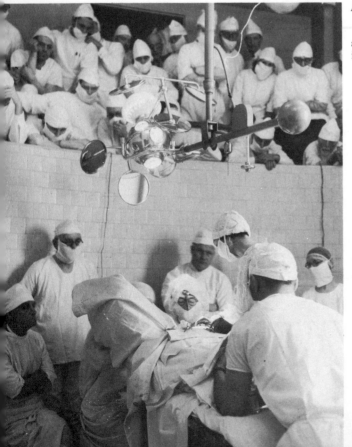

DR. RAFE C. CHAFFIN was observed performing a delicate operation at the California Hospital, now the California Hospital Medical Center, in 1934. By means of a tiny microphone concealed in his sanitary mask, Dr. Chaffin explained the steps in the operation over a public address system. Watching the operation were members of the American College of Surgeons. (CHMC)

TERMINAL ISLAND, once the playground of the very wealthy, was claimed in the Depression era by squatters living in broken down shacks and old wooden-frame houses in a city nick-named "Squatters' Village." In 1935, they were ordered to move, however, to make way for a new yacht harbor. About fifty families, mostly elderly seafaring people, were affected. (H-E)

OUT FOR A TRIAL RUN before the Transpacific Yacht Race in 1934 was the schooner *Scaramouche*. The yacht was one of twelve entries in the 2,225-mile race between San Pedro and Diamond Head in Honolulu, Hawaii. Skippered by William Tomkins, the 43-foot long boat sailed under the colors of the Long Beach Yacht Club.

THOUSANDS CHEERED Pres. Franklin Delano Roosevelt when he toured Los Angeles in 1935 at the height of the economic depression in the United States. At that time, Roosevelt was known for his "New Deal" and for his "fireside chats," broadcast over radio to the nation, which helped explain his policies and issues. In this picture at the Los Angeles Memorial Coliseum, where he was greeted by about 70,000 persons, he spoke from his automobile while surrounded by newspaper men, newsreel cameras, and security guards. Roosevelt was in the back seat with his wife Eleanor, and Mayor Frank L. Shaw of Los Angeles.

LELAND ANDREWS, an American Airlines pilot flew this American Airlines Vultee on February 20, 1935, nonstop from Glendale's Grand Central Airport to New York City's Floyd Bennett Field. Andrews, a World War I pilot, flew by way of Washington, D.C., and established a record of 11 hours, 34 minutes, and 16 seconds for transcontinental flight. On the same flight, Andrews also broke the nonstop record to Washington, passing over the city after 10 hours, 22 minutes, and 54 seconds. (American)

THE AL G. BARNES CIRCUS, which had winter quarters in the Los Angeles area, made it a practice for many years to perform before the crippled children of the Orthopaedic Hospital. In 1935, elephants entertained the children as well as a large crowd of spectators at Flower near Twenty-fourth Street, right in the middle of the street, where traffic always was blocked off for the event.

[161]

PAST EIGHTY AND FOUR HUSBANDS later, the legendary "Silver Queen" of Pasadena, Susanna Bransford Emery Holmes Delitch Engath-cheff, in 1935 said she wouldn't mind getting married again, providing she met the right man. Her millions came from her first husband, A. B. Emery, from whom she inherited the Silver King silver mines at Park City, Utah. (H-E)

THE LOS ANGELES CIVIC CHORUS of 350 voices gave its first annual concert in Trinity Auditorium on July 10, 1936, with J. Arthur Lewis as director. Founded and organized by Lewis, the director of the 1932 Olympiad Chorus, the group was self-sustaining. Members paid monthly dues, bought their own music, and furnished their own uniforms. The chorus operated under the sponsorship of the Los Angeles Recreation and Parks Department, and was by City Council proclamation the official Los Angeles chorus. It appeared on civic and festive occasions, and performed on radio across the country. (Fraggi)

A NEW ERA OF PROGRESS was signaled for Los Angeles and other Southern California communities in 1936 with the arrival of the first electric power from Boulder Dam, 266 miles away. One-hundred-and-fifty large searchlights helped throw millions of candlepower of light down the length of Broadway, while marchers and floats paraded up the street from Olympic Boulevard. Thousands of people turned out to see the criss-crossing of the searchlight beams, to cheer the historic event, and to witness the turning of night into day. (H-E)

MORE THAN 150,000 spectators lined the sidewalks and streets to cheer 10,000 Elks, marchers and riders, in 1936 during the group's annual convention in Los Angeles. Here the parade reached Seventh Street and Broadway, with the float entered by Florida Elk's lodges in foreground. Bands, as well as floats and automobiles, paraded through the downtown streets. (H-E)

CARGOES WERE TIED UP in holds, and ships were brought to a standstill when various sea unions struck in 1936. This row in Los Angeles' outer harbor was part of the 117 ships idled in Los Angeles alone, and part of the 150 that were standing silently in different harbors up and down the Pacific Coast. Some 37,000 marine workers, including fishermen, took part in the walkout. (H-E)

FIVE UNITED STATES ARMY VETERANS were buried in 1936 before relatives and friends, with complete military honors, at the National Military Home cemetery at Sawtelle. The men who died were: John E. Hess, private, United States Volunteer Infantry, Philippines; William E. Watts, private, First North Dakota Volunteer Infantry, Spanish-American War; Oliver P. McCoy, private, First Oregon Volunteer Infantry, Spanish-American War; Charles C. Hinds, corporal, medical corps, World War I; and Maurice Van de Velde, wagoner, 316th United States Engineers, World War I. After the funeral, relatives were given the flags that had decorated the tops of the caskets. (H-E)

[165]

ANY KIND OF SPORT INVOLVING AUTOMOBILES developed a following in Los Angeles—and auto polo was no exception. What made the sport exciting to watch were the swirling, charging, bumping cars, and the lumps the players took. Here two specially adapted vehicles practiced for an upcoming match at Los Angeles Memorial Coliseum during an American Legion fireworks show and circus in 1937.

THE LOS ANGELES MEMORIAL COLISEUM was lit up like a Christmas tree for a sensational electrical pageant sponsored by the Elks, who were holding a convention in Los Angeles in 1936. This unusual parade climaxed four days of meetings that had brought 50,000 Elks to Los Angeles. The shimmering, gorgeously lit floats were entered in the parade by motion picture studios and civic groups, and were lined up around the Coliseum track as a crowd of some 80,000 Elks and residents cheered.

THIS POLO TEAM, which competed under Los Angeles Athletic Club colors, represented the United States in the 1936 Olympic Games in Berlin, Germany. Members of the team, in bathing suits, were, kneeling (left to right), Wallace O'Connor, Phillip Daubenspeck, Kenneth Beck, and Frank Graham. Standing were, Charles Finn, Harold McCallister, Calvert Strong, and Herbert Wildman. The team's coach, Clyde Swendsen, is kneeling at left. The rest are unidentified. (H-E)

ALTHOUGH LAW ENFORCEMENT OFFICIALS of Los Angeles County worked mainly within a man's world in 1937, they harbored no prejudices against women. Here Sheriff Eugene Biscailuz swore in two women as deputies, Doris Kirkeby (left), a social worker with a degree from USC, and Vivienne Crumley, who majored in psychology and sociology at UCLA. (LACSD)

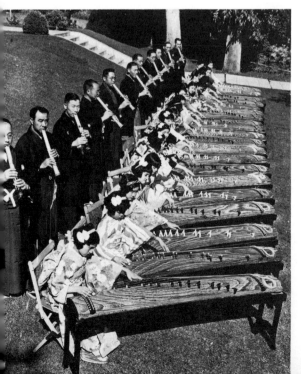

YOUNG JAPANESE GIRLS warmed up the harps while the men played the "Shakuhachi," flutes, in preparation for a colorful Japanese musical festival that opened in an outdoor park theater in Los Angeles in 1937. The collection of harps called "Koto," was the greatest ever shown in America. (H-E)

[167]

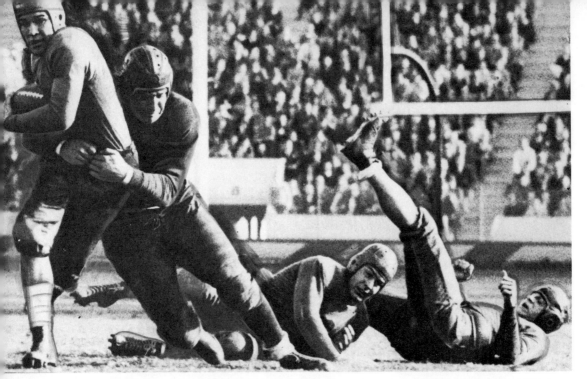

FOOTBALL FANS LOVED the Los Angeles Bulldogs when they freelanced in the middle 1930s. Owned by Professional Sports Enterprises, the team competed against barnstorming clubs from the National Football League and the American Football League. Its advisory board included Joe E. Brown, George Raft, Bing Crosby, and Earl B. Gilmore. At this game against the Rochester Tigers at Gilmore Stadium in 1937, more than 17,000 hysterical fans jammed the ball park to see the Bulldogs crush the Tigers 48 to 21, although on this play the Bulldogs were temporarily stalled. Here Davie Davis, a substitute quarterback and former USC star, missed a bad pass from center and was tackled by the Tigers in the shadow of his own goal line. Other players on the team included Frank Greene, Roy Berry, Gordon Dore, Dan Barnhart, Pete Mehringer, and Ike Frankien. (Alcana)

[168]

WOMEN HAD THEIR OPPORTUNITY to compete with men even in 1938, particularly if they wanted to learn how to train lions and tigers. A school operated by Mabel Stark in Baldwyn Park at the winter quarters of the Al G. Barnes-Sells Floto Circus opened with two pupils, and many applicants. Here Miss Stark (left) introduces one of her students, Marion Royce, to the lions. Supposedly the school was a roaring success. (H-E)

A HOLLYWOOD PREMIERE always brought out huge, cheering crowds, photographers, studio officials, parking attendants, lights, and a long red carpet for the stars. *Wee Willie Winkle* was no exception when it was premiered near Beverly Hills in 1937 at the Carthay Circus Theater. Thousands of movie fans arrived early for a choice vantage position and waited all day for a glimpse of the film's stars. Shirley Temple and Victor McLaglen. (Twentieth)

A DRENCHING RAIN that fell on Southern California in 1938 couldn't keep these movie fans from trying to catch a glimpse of their favorite stars as they lined up eagerly for the "press preview" of the film *Kentucky*, outside the Carthay Circle Theater. This was the last of the big press previews that were held with the arching sky lights and lots of hoopla. Afterwards, press previews were scheduled for behind the studio walls. (H-E)

THE FEDERAL THEATERS PROJECT, which arose out of the Depression, offered relief work and jobs to many unemployed actors and actresses in the theatrical profession. This picture shows a gathering of the chorus line of one of the federal productions, *Ready, Aim, Fire,* which opened in 1937.

HOWARD HUGHES was an avid pilot in his early years, and in 1935 and 1937 set world speed marks in his Hughes Racer. During his later years, Hughes went out of his way to shun the public and retain his privacy, living in strict, guarded seclusion while running his vast industrial empire from secret hideouts. (H-E)

HUNDREDS OF LOS ANGELES HOUSEWIVES left their families in 1938 to participate in the city's annual "Play Day" at Griffith Park playground, where they took part in games, gymnastics, dancing, and singing. The purpose of play day, according to the Los Angeles Department of Recreation and Parks, was to demonstrate to the women all the leisure pursuits available to them. Some eight hundred women throughout the day arrived at the playground with tennis rackets, volleyballs, baseball bats, swim suits, and picnic lunches. (H-E)

[171]

YOUNGSTERS of the Tenth Street Elementary School left behind all books, tests, and lessons as they raced from classrooms for their summer vacation period in 1938. The exhuberant youths joined with 300,000 others who streamed from schools on June 23, the last day until sometime in September. Teachers, too, were happy to join in the mass exodus. (H-E)

LOS ANGELES joined the nation in 1938 in celebrating Flag Day on the 161st anniversary of the formal acceptance of the stars and stripes by the United States. The event was marked here when an American flag was raised on the site of Fort Moore, the military post established in Los Angeles when the city was first settled by Americans. Raising the flag was W. H. Cobb, and to his right, in a white dress, was Clara Hughes, who sang the national anthem. Mrs. F. B. Harrington, in white dress on the base of the flagpole, was flag chairman of the State Society of the Daughters of 1812, which sponsored the ceremony. (H-E)

DARINGLY "COPASETIC" was this female "jitterbug" who did a split just as good as any pro. Although Los Angeles nightclub owners in 1938 frowned on these "alligators" for "shining," the young dancers had their way. "Jitterbugs" in those days had a language that was all their own, and spurned sweet and sentimental music as being too "schmaltzy" or "corny." (H-E)

BOYS WILL BE BOYS, as Los Angeles Mayor Fletcher Bowron proved in 1938 when he was initiated into the Los Angeles Breakfast Club. Blindfolded, and riding the famous Ham horse, Bowron dipped his hand into a plate of ham and eggs as part of the ritual. With Bowron were left to right, Harold B. Link, club manager; Judge William R. McKay; Bowron; and G. E. Moreland, club president.

THE CITY'S FINEST ARMISTICE DAY PARADE took place in 1938 before a record-breaking throng, as 15,000 persons marched down Broadway and honored the war dead and the twentieth anniversary of the signing of World War I's armistice. These former troops marched to City Hall, where they passed in review before military and civic officials. (H-E)

THE MIDWICK COUNTRY Club, now a golf course, was located in the Alhambra area from about the 1920s to 1950. The club had two polo fields, a grandstand, and a large scoreboard, and featured some of the best polo played in the United States at the time. Not only did the best players from the West and East coasts compete there, but so did teams that represented other countries. (CSAF)

NED SPARKS, who became famous as a grouch in films, and whose half-chewed cigar was his trademark, applied in 1939 for a Lloyd's of London insurance policy guaranteeing him $10,000 if any photograph was published that showed him smiling. With Sparks was Thatcher Taylor, his agent. The sour-faced comedian successfully made millions of moviegoers laugh simply with a frozen scowl and a rasping voice. His humorless film portrayals weren't the real man. Friends knew him as a warm and sympathetic human being.

THE ROARING MIDGETS in the 1930s and 1940s used to thrill sell-out, weeknight crowds at Gilmore Stadium, located at what is now the southeast corner of Beverly Boulevard and Fairfax Avenue. In this 1938 picture, Reynold Coleman was caught crashing into the stadium's north wall, but got out of the jam without serious injury. Loie Ulbrich was in the car on the ground.

LOS ANGELES RESIDENTS discovered the joys of walking the trails of their city's hills and mountains in the summer of 1939. They also found it was more exhilarating to hike in groups than singly. Since Los Angeles that year was a relatively wide open city, with the great housing boom of the post-war years yet to come, there were miles and miles of ground for hikers to explore. (Shanfeld)

GOLFER JIMMY DEMERET started fast and finished hot when he won the 1939 Los Angeles Open golf tournament at Griffith Park by seven strokes over Jug McSpaden. Demeret toured the 72 holes in a 274, one shot off the Los Angeles Open record. The last day saw Demeret chipping over wires from the gallery back of the 18th green on one of his shots. (H-E)

HARNESS RACES at the Los Angeles County Fair at Pomona started in 1922 when the sulkies ran on Sunday afternoons in "no betting" contests. Purses of $200 to $500, however, were awarded the owners of winning horses. By the time this picture was taken in 1939, legalized betting was in effect, and the harness horses were playing second fiddle to the thoroughbreds. (CSAF)

PINE NEEDLE SKIING turned out to be nothing more than a big fad in 1939 when Sepp Benedikter, a former Austrian ski expert who originated the idea, gave lessons on a hill at Ventura and Lankershim boulevards. Under a warming sun, interested skiers learned on needles, imported from the High Sierras, piled from one to two inches deep. The skis were specially made, with no wax and no steel edges. (Alcana)

UNION STATION was introduced to Los Angeles in 1939 with a gala three-day party that cost approximately $30,000. The $11-million station, located near the Plaza on Alameda Street, served the Southern Pacific, Santa Fe, and Union Pacific railroads. Sixty trains and some seven thousand passengers were accommodated daily following its dedication on May 3. (H-E)

COLORS AND BANNERS of the various Los Angeles locals of the American Federation of Labor were massed on the steps of City Hall in 1939 following a Labor Day parade. They flanked labor and public officials who had turned out to review the procession. Congress of Industrial Organizations' units also paraded that day. (H-E)

THESE DANCERS AND TROUBADORS took part in the annual San Gabriel Fiesta hald in San Gabriel in September 1939. On the palomino horses were Annette Crockette, who led the fiesta parade on her mount, "El Morino," and Jack Davis, who rode "Beau Brummel," a three-year-old blue-ribbon stallion.

WHEN LOS ANGELES' NEW TERMINAL ANNEX POST OFFICE opened in 1940 south of Union Station on Alameda Street, it was the largest mail handling facility in the West. The building was of ultra-modern design on the inside, but featured a Spanish-type architecture for its facade. After its opening, when it was fully staffed, more than two thousand persons worked there.

[178]

THE COLLEGE OF DENTISTRY of the University of Southern California was serving 25,000 persons annually in its big clinic room by 1940. This picture shows a part of the clinic, where 58 students worked at the same time. Here some 320 students were able to gain practical experience before graduation; and patients, who couldn't afford regular dentists, were able to get treatment for almost nothing. (USC)

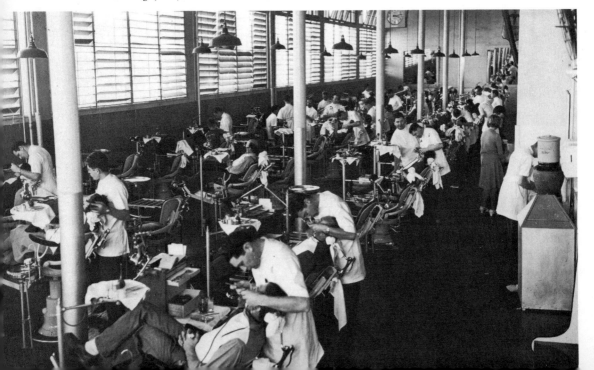

War and Peace:
1940 to 1950

WITH WAR CLOUDS hovering overhead, and prosperity in its future, Los Angeles moved into the 1940s. It was an uncertain time. Poland and France fell to the Germans, and President Roosevelt urgently attempted to boost defense by requesting 50,000 more airplanes, over a third of which were to be built by factories in Los Angeles County. Local manufacturers, with large contracts in hand, began hiring by the thousands, and from across the nation a stream of people once again rushed to Los Angeles for jobs in the aviation industry.

The nation talked of peace with Japan, and the first water from the Colorado River flowed across the state via aqueducts to Los Angeles. The Pasadena Freeway, forerunner of a vast superhighway system, opened between downtown Los Angeles and Pasadena.

Angelenos queued up in long lines with the rest of the nation to watch Clark Gable and Vivien Leigh in *Gone With the Wind*, and bought record numbers of newspapers, reading with relish about the juicy scandals emanating from the movie colony.

Shortly after Pearl Harbor, Errol Flynn was accused by a seventeen-year-old girl of statutory rape. With Jerry Geisler defending him, Flynn was acquitted, and came out of the trial a bigger star than ever. Geisler later defended Charlie Chaplin, who first went before a Grand Jury when a young actress called him the father of her unborn child. The Grand Jury believed Charlie and let him go. After the baby was born, however, Chaplin was prosecuted anyway, lost, and had to pay $100 a month for child support. Although Hollywood was airing its dirty linen in public, the industry, nevertheless, was essential to the war effort. The federal government said movies were good propaganda vehicles and morale boosters, and froze workers at studios in their jobs until war's end.

The attack on Pearl Harbor shocked and panicked the nation. As a result, the local Japanese were pushed into relocation centers, whether they liked it or not. They were stripped of their property, deprived of their legal rights, and were imprisoned without a trial. It was one of the most shameful acts in the history of the country. Other minorities also were troubled, although not directly, because of the war. When Mexican-Americans in zoot-suits walked the downtown streets, they were attacked by irate servicemen while police looked the other way, and *pachucos* were arrested only because they looked suspicious and sported tattoos.

The war ended, and manufacturing employment shriveled. By the late 1940s, the aircraft industry shifted to electronics instead of airplanes, and saw its future in the development of missiles and anti-missiles.

Then came the biggest boom ever. Subdividers bought up land and began putting up row after row of brightly colored tract homes. Builders offered long-term loans, low down payments, and even no down payments. War workers and former servicemen who had saved their money rushed to buy. It wasn't long before the city's population climbed to 1.5 million. Inch by inch, foot by foot, grudgingly, farms and orange groves disappeared. Houses sprang up where cows once munched contentedly. Instead of the groves, long rows of box-like homes lined newly laid-out streets. Within a few years, Los Angeles found itself devoid of its wide-open spaces. Developers then turned to the San Fernando Valley, and more and more communities were constructed. The hammer and saw ruled the land.

Critics said Los Angeles was a community of suburbs in search of a city. They were right. No longer was it a green garden, a flowery, pastoral land. Instead, it had become urbanized, congested, sprawling, reaching out in all directions.

Smog hit finally with great force. People cried and shed tears, and the state formed the Los Angeles County Air Pollution Control District. Sulphur dioxide was spewing into the air. Officials moved against oil refineries, steam plants, and factories, but the smog continued, despite the studies and the new rules.

Once in their new homes, Angelenos shut themselves in before their new television sets. They sat in their living rooms, while a lot of movie-house owners fumed and went broke. To sell tickets, the movie industry came up with the wide screen, stereophonic sound, three dimensions, and giveaways. Nothing helped very much.

The youth of the city grew taller, stronger, and healthier, and jammed the beaches to sun, swim, and surf. Life was all water and sand, and the bikini-clad California girls, with long, straight blonde hair and blue eyes, became more fact than fiction. The boosters pulled out the old drums and beat out messages which called attention to a sporty, industrious, recreational, and sunny California. Los Angeles, which had never stopped growing, was on its way to becoming the nation's fourth largest city.

BABY SANDY was a big movie star by the time she was two years old and able to climb up on a chair to blow out the candles on her birthday cake in 1940. The Hollywood toddler was dairyman Roy Henville's daughter, who cooed her way to fame in the movies. (H-E)

THOUSANDS OF CHILDREN from kindergarten to high school age rode colorful miniature floats in Alhambra's fourth annual Story Book parade in 1940. The winner of the parade's sweepstakes prize, "Babies Boat—The Silver Moon," entered by the Garfield Elementary School, is seen moving down the city's main street in front of thousands of spectators. (H-E)

HOLLYWOOD PARK RACE TRACK in Inglewood drew many socialites in 1940 before the United States entered World War II. On a tour of the track's spacious grounds were Junior Leaguers, left to right, Julia Dockweiler, Eleanor Anton, Virginia Anton, and Mrs. Dodge Dunning. During the war years, Hollywood Park, along with other tracks around the country, closed at the request of the federal government, which was fearful that the races siphoned off great sums of money that the defense workers were earning. (Bayrd)

LOS ANGELES was where the U.S. Army Recruiting Service first introduced its mobile recruiting van, a new one and one half-ton truck. Receiving enlistment applications from a group of young men in front of the Federal Building in 1940 were Capt. Arthur Davidson, in truck, and Lt. Phillip Crowell, standing. (USA)

BEVERLY HILLS' INITIAL MANPOWER QUOTA under the Selective Service Act of 1940 was filled when these nine men volunteered for army duty. Pictured in a civic ceremony before dignitaries at Beverly Hills City Hall they are, left to right, Tom Hampson, Bert Cloos, Mel Grau, Mal Robertson, Ernest Pearson, Carl Pearson, Reuben Carrillo, James J. Tracey, and Victor W. Kline, Jr. Immediately after the ceremonies, the young men left for the army induction center, where they were all sworn in. (H-E)

APPROXIMATELY 500,000 articles of clothing were turned out monthly by women of the Work Project Administration for people on relief in Los Angeles. This sewing group in 1940 made the clothes in up-to-date styles so that needy persons could present a good front when out on job interviews.

JOE E. BROWN, the comedian with the big mouth, returned to the musical comedy stage in 1941 as the star of *Rio Rita,* a Civic Light Opera presentation at the Philharmonic Auditorium. Brown, who started in the silent movies in 1927, made twenty-four films during his Hollywood career. He was known as an "All-American guy" who loved kids and baseball, and was one of the first of the stars to travel overseas to entertain the troops during World War II. (H-E)

HOWARD HUGHES (right), an eccentric businessman and a pilot during his lifetime, was once an enthusiastic filmmaker. During his Hollywood career, he was probably the most publicized ladies' man—linked romantically with such names as Jean Harlow, Billy Dove, Katharine Hepburn, Jane Russell, Olivia DeHavilland, Lana Turner, Ava Gardner, and Jean Peters. Here, in 1941, he directs actor Walter Huston in a scene from *The Outlaw,* which he also produced. Hughes was producer and director for the enormously successful *Hell's Angels,* and produced *The Front Page* and *Scarface.* (H-E)

HEAVY RAINS caused such runoffs in Los Angeles in 1941 that some car drivers literally had to get a horse. In some intersections of the city, water stood three and four feet deep, following a downpour that brought more than 3.14 inches of rain. Cars were imprisoned by mud and water, and streets and roads looked like this in the San Fernando Valley and other sections of the city. (H-E)

BEACHFRONT HOMES in Redondo Beach had been battered by huge waves in 1941, and their owners worked feverishly day and night filling potato sacks with sand for a barricade. Though parts of the beachfront city were protected by a wall of sandbags, officials of the Army Corps of Engineers were afraid that many more dwellings would be claimed by the sea. (H-E)

LOS ANGELES HARBOR SHIPYARDS, just before the start of World War II in 1941, were busy working on a program that called for the building of 1,400 ships nationally, as suggested by the United States Maritime Commission. Ships taking form in the harbor, from left to right, were the S.S. *Agwiprince,* the S.S. *Alcoa Polaris,* and the S.S. *Alcoa Pennant.* In those months before Pearl Harbor, shipbuilding here was way ahead of schedule. (LAHD)

[184]

THE BODY of Councilman Evan Lewis lay in state with a guard of honor in the rotunda of City Hall, where associates and civic leaders paid him tribute in 1941. Lewis had died in his home of a lingering heart ailment after serving for twelve years as a councilman. He first became a councilman in 1928 when he was appointed to fill the post left open by Frank L. Shaw, who had been elected to the Board of Supervisors, and who later became mayor of Los Angeles. Lewis was noted for his booming voice, and his attacks against the administrations of mayors George E. Cryer, John C. Porter, Shaw, and Fletcher Bowron. He led fights against graft in city government, against special assessments, and against special interest groups and lobbyists. (H-E)

[185]

DRESSED IN COLORFUL JAPANESE COSTUMES, the queen and her court of the eighth annual Nisei Festival held in Little Tokyo, visited various Los Angeles city offices and businesses in 1941 calling attention to the event as part of the pre-festival spirit. The royal group included Queen Reiko Inouye, seated; and, left to right, Maye Noma, Shizuyo Ishino, Dorothy Iijima, and Masa Fujioka.

PANICKY LOS ANGELES OFFICIALS, even before Pearl Harbor in 1941, thought these Japanese fishermen at Fish Harbor, Terminal Island, would turn their vessels into torpedo boats, and would blow up important defense positions on the West Coast. The officials claimed that many of the fishing boats were operated by Japanese naval reservists, who often held military drill when their boats were out at sea. After the war started, however, none of these claims turned out to be true. (H-E)

SUPERIOR COURT JUDGE EDWARD R. BRAND (left) and Los Angeles County Clerk John F. Moroney dipped into the Grand Jury wheel in 1942 for names of residents to be considered for Grand Jury duty. The county officials picked thirty names out of which only nineteen were chosen to serve. (H-E)

GIRLS HAD TO VOLUNTEER to harvest the crops in the San Fernando Valley in 1942 as all the men were in the armed forces. In preparation, members of the American Women's Voluntary Services were shown how to sort out peaches by Joe Maromarco, who in those days had the biggest peach orchard in the San Fernando Valley. The girls were, left to right, Mrs. Helen Barnard, and Misses Shirley Garman, Jane Smith, Ann Evans, and Mary Nored. (Universal)

U.S. ARMY dive bombers fly over Santa Monica in 1941 just before the start of World War II. The two-seated, all-metal monoplanes, manufactured by the Douglas Aircraft Company, were almost identical to the planes Douglas was delivering to the Navy. (Douglas)

VOLUNTEERS for the American Women's Voluntary Services, North Hollywood Branch, signed up in 1942. They were, seated left to right, actress Janet Gaynor, Mrs. Paul MacWilliams, and Maris Wrixon. Overlooking the signees were members, left to right, Naney Coleman, Mrs. Pat O'Brien, Mrs. Frank McHugh, Alexis Smith, Mrs. Bill Sexton, and Mrs. Bob Hope, who was chairman of the North Hollywood group.

SPACE FOR MILITARY ACTIVITIES on the home front became scarce in Los Angeles after Pearl Harbor. One of the places where candidates were interviewed for cadet training in the United States Army Air Corps in 1942 was at an old mansion at 611 South Ardmore Avenue. The aviation cadet examining board consisted of Lt. Lester Blount, Robert L. Woods, and Ned P. Eads.

[187]

THE SERVICE FLAG with 305 stars flew from the top of the Los Angeles Department of Water and Power's Municipal Utility Building at 207 South Broadway in 1942. Each star represented a Department of Water and Power employe who had entered a branch of the nation's armed forces. At ceremonies prior to the unfurling of the flag were, to the right of the flag, Clinton E. Miller, president of the board of water and power commissioners; and A. M. Patton, to Miller's right, president of the Employe Association. (H-E)

[188]

LOS ANGELES NISEI, second-generation Japanese who were American citizens, formally organised and pledged their "all-out energy to defeat Japan and the Axis" in 1942. These four girls added their names to a petition to Pres. Franklin Delano Roosevelt, reaffirming their allegiance to the United States. They were, left to right, Sadac Momura, Martha Kaihatsu, Coralee Inoshita, and Margaret Matsumot. (H-E)

SMOG TROUBLED Los Angeles even in the early 1940s, as this picture of the downtown section indicates. One of the worst smogs in history turned day into night, and caused citizens to besiege the Los Angeles City Council with requests for a complete investigation into causes and corrective measures. The gaseous, eye-smarting fumes not only covered the city's business area, but also struck many suburban communities as well.

ALL SERVICEMEN ON LEAVE in Los Angeles could have eaten all the turkey they wanted on Thanksgiving Day in 1943 as various organizations opened their doors and played host to these veterans. This was a typical scene throughout the city as the Christian Service Center made it a "happy" Thanksgiving for 1,000 soldiers, sailors, Marines, merchant marines, and men of the Air Force at the center on Cahuenga Boulevard in Hollywood. (H-E)

A PROCESSION OF PRIESTS moved into Saint Paul's Cathedral for Holy Communion marking the opening of the 49th annual conclave of the Los Angeles Episcopal Diocese on January 26, 1944. Saint Paul's had its beginning in 1865 when a small group met in Los Angeles' Wells Fargo Express office under the direction of an Episcopal priest from Indiana. As a result of the meeting, Saint Athanasius, the first Protestant church in Los Angeles and the forerunner of Saint Paul's, was erected at High and Temple streets, now the Civic Center. In 1883, the name was changed to Saint Paul's. (H-E)

[190]

ONE OF THESE TEN HIGH SCHOOL BEAUTIES became queen of downtown Los Angeles in 1944 in a contest sponsored by the Businessmen's Association. They were, left to right, Tracy Burchard, Leone Johnson, Sally Applegate, Betty Duncan, Mary Lewis, Virginia Jung, Shirley Merkle, Lillian Kassan, Shirley Kay Feddersen, and Donna Blaine. (H-E)

MORE THAN 250,000 SPECTATORS lined the downtown streets in 1944 to watch a display of America's military strength prior to an Army-Navy show in the Los Angeles Memorial Coliseum that evening. The parade, witnessed by the largest crowd ever to gather for this kind of an event, also was reviewed by generals, admirals, and other military leaders. (H-E)

VETERANS WEREN'T FORGOTTEN on Memorial Day 1943, when ceremonies were held to honor the dead of all wars. In a typical scene throughout the Southland, the Drum, Fife, and Bugle Corps of Theodore Roosevelt Camp No. 9, Spanish-American War Veterans, led the parade at Rosedale Cemetery.

REAL WAR GAMES were played by these women at a "filter center" in 1943 at a secret location somewhere in Los Angeles. Known as the Aircraft Warning Corps, the women took in information of planes and locations from thousands of spotters in Southern California. Afterward, the information was relayed to the area's military officials, who could then determine whether or not Los Angeles should be alerted. (H-E)

HOLLYWOOD'S BOND CAVALCADE returned home after a 10,091-mile railroad trip through fifteen cities to sell war bonds, and was greeted by more than three thousand cheering fans at the Southern Pacific railroad station in Glendale. The stars sold $1,079,586,819 in bonds from coast to coast in 1943. Kneeling, left to right, were Sully Mason, Muriel Goodspeed, Harpo Marx, Julie Conway, Doris Merrick, Mickey Rooney, Rosemary LaPlanche, Margie Stewart, and Diana Pendleton. Standing, left to right, were Kenneth Thomson (tour manager), Ruth Brady, Dorothy Merritt, Kathryn Grayson, Betty Hutton, Ish Kabibble, Lucille Ball, Howard D. Mills (regional director of the War Finance Committee), Greer Garson, Kay Kyser, Georgia Carroll, Jose Iturbi, Fred Astaire, Judy Garland, and Dick Powell.

THE FORTIETH LIBERTY SHIP launched by the California Shipbuilding Corporation at Terminal Island was sent on its way with traditional ceremonies in 1943. Completing the honors by smashing the champagne bottle was Mrs. Frank Higbee, wife of Lt. Cmdr. Frank D. Higbee, captain of the port of Los Angeles and member of the U.S. Coast Guard. Miss Anne Higbee stood behind her mother as maid of honor; and another daughter, Joan, held the roses just below the launching platform. (LAHD)

LOS ANGELES MEN between 45 and 65 years of age also were called to war, and signed up in 1942 at one of the Selective Service stations located at 8883 West Pico Boulevard. Approximately 150,000 senior men who saw duty on the home front were registered. (H-E)

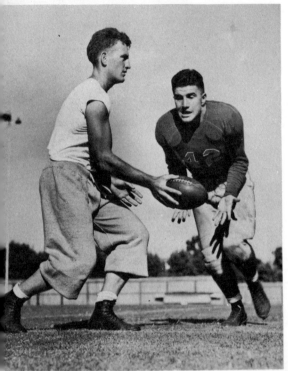

ALTHOUGH THE NATION WAS AT WAR, football continued to be a morale booster, and many eyes, civilian as well as military, continued to focus on the college teams. At UCLA Lt. Bob Waterfield (the great quarterback who led the Bruins to the Rose Bowl where they lost to Georgia 9-0) worked out with his successor, Bob Andrews, a reserve on the 1942 Stanford team, in preparation for the 1943 season. A Navy trainee, Andrews was one of UCLA's stars that year. (UCLA)

SHERMAN TANKS and other military equipment rolled through the streets of downtown Los Angeles in 1943 to promote the nation's third war-loan bond drive during World War II. Thousands of spectators lined the sidewalks to watch the parade, and afterwards aided the war effort by buying billions of dollars worth of bonds—first sold as defense bonds in 1941. Buyers considered bonds the safest investment in the world, and everyone loyal to the United States in those years managed to buy at least one.

MEMBERS OF THE FIRST BATTALION of the Second Filipino Regiment, carrying their famous bolo knives, marched in a parade in 1943 to celebrate the eighth anniversary of the establishment of the Commonwealth of the Philippines. The United States recognized the independence of the Philippines on July 4, 1946. (H-E)

SCORES OF BOFORS 40 MM ANTI-AIRCRAFT gun mounts and carriages rolled along to final assembly in 1942 at the Firestone Tire and Rubber Company plant. Also in production at the factory was a new type of barrage balloon, one of which can be seen in the background. To produce the gun mounts and carriages, Firestone had to build a five-acre factory, and organize a skilled force of 1,500 machinists and other workers. (Firestone)

LONG BEACH WAS TYPICAL of many large cities in California on V-J Day, August 14, 1945, when servicemen exchanged kisses with every girl available. There were parades in the streets, dancing, drinking, flag waving, shouting, cheering, and general tumult. The news that World War II had ended, and that Japan had accepted Allied surrender terms set off celebrations that lasted all day and night. From windows of office buildings, ticker-tape and confetti rained down on the crowds; ship whistles, automobile horns, and sirens blasted away. Thousands of shipyard workers yelled, tossed their hats into the air, and walked off their jobs. Coast Guard and fire boats sounded their steam whistles, and at Fort MacArthur, scores of rounds of 155-millimeter shells were fired. (LB)

ONE OF THE MOST IMPRESSIVE of Easter services was conducted on Catalina Island in 1946. Carrying torches, and dressed as early-day pilgrims, these residents climbed a steep hill to get to the top of Mount Buena Vista, where the services were held before hundreds of viewers overlooking Avalon Bay and the Avalon Casino. (H-E)

CONTROVERSIAL INDUSTRIALIST and billionaire Howard Hughes is shown in the cockpit of his giant "Spruce Goose" flying boat in Long Beach harbor in 1947. The largest airplane ever built of wood (because of the scarcity of metal during World War II), it had a 320-foot wingspan, weighed 200 tons, and was eight stories tall. With Hughes at the controls, it flew only once for about a mile, and never went higher than three or four feet above the water. The giant plywood ship was designed to carry 700 soldiers over an ocean. Eventually it was acquired by the Smithsonian Institute. (H-E)

MAJOR LEAGUE BASEBALL and major league press agentry combined at the opening of 1946 spring practice at Pasadena's Brookside Park, where the American League's Chicago White Sox were encamped. Infielder Dario Lodigiani went along with the gag, and slid into third base as actress Peggy Knudsen leaped into the air to catch a high throw. With antics like this, who cared if Lodigiani wasn't tagged out! (H-E)

CLOAKED IN PURPLE VESTMENTS and wearing the white pallium symbolic of the bishopric, the body of the Most Reverend John J. Cantwell lay in state in November 1947 in the sanctuary of Saint Vibiana's Cathedral. Archbishop Cantwell, leader of the Catholic Archdiocese for Los Angeles, died at the Queen of Angels Hospital from a "strep" throat infection. Inscribed in Latin on the casket was the archbishop's name, his archdiocese, and the dates of his birth and death—"Ioannes Ioseph Cantwell— archiepiscopus angelorem—1874-1947." Of forged bronze, the canton-crepe-lined casket was too heavy for the pallbearers, weighing 1,700 pounds. The prelate, Los Angeles' seventh bishop, was buried at Calvary Cemetery. (H-E)

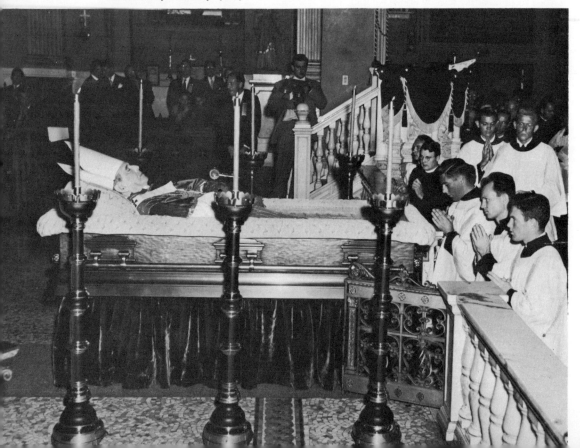

THE BIG DEBATE over which is faster—a quarter horse or a thoroughbred—was finally solved on August 4, 1947, when Barbara B, an Arizona-owned quarter horse, beat Fair Truckle, a thoroughbred, in a quarter-mile match race at Hollywood Park Race Track. Each horse owner put up $50,000 for the winner-take-all purse of $100,000. The race was held in the late morning on a Monday, following the close of the Hollywood Park season. Thousands of fans, attending the race free, saw jockey Frank Licata on Barbara B win over Johnny Longden on Fair Truckle by two lengths in 21 3/5 seconds. (H-E)   [199]

GOING ON A TRAIN RIDE was part of the educational experience, even in Duarte in 1948. Here, fourth-grade students from the Duarte Elementary School wave to the engineer of an oncoming Santa Fe train as it pulls into the Monrovia station to take them on a tour. This train, No. 42, was used for the San Bernardino run, a local route. (H-E)

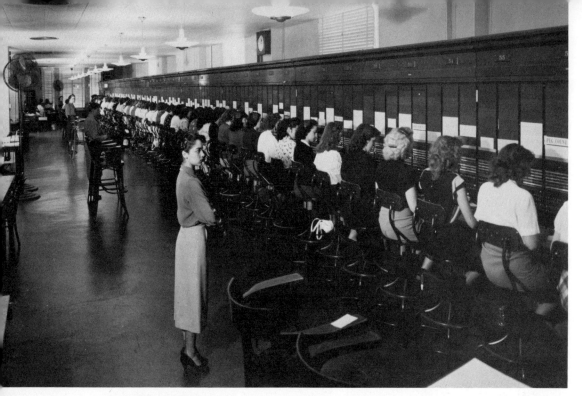

MORE THAN 57,500 DAILY CALLS were handled by a staff of 244 operators from a switchboard in the telephone office at 433 South Olive Street in 1948. These Pacific Telephone operators served more than 100,000 telephones in downtown Los Angeles. (Bayrd)

[200] "LAS POSADAS," Mexico's traditional eight-day Christmas celebration, was colorfully reenacted in miniature at Pershing Square in 1949. Highlight of the event was the breaking of the large, star-shaped "pinata," which was filled with candy and small gifts. Portraying the three wise men were, left to right, Mexican Vice-consul Porfirio A. Romay, Enrique Oretega, and Juana de Romenico. The three children were, left to right, Salvador Yosio, Maria Teresa Yosio, and Raul Gutierrez Yosio, Santa Claus was unidentified. (H-E)

WHEN THREE-AND-ONE-HALF-YEAR-OLD Kathy Fiscus fell into the pipe of an abandoned water well near her home in San Marino in 1949, the entire nation tuned in on rescue operations, and five thousand spectators flooded the site to watch. For 54 hours, men and machines worked to save the child trapped about ninety-five feet below the earth's surface. When they found her, she was dead. Here, O. A. Kelly, a machinist, is lowered into the rescue shaft during a phase of the operation. The disaster turned Los Angeles residents on to television as they never had been before. Interest in the tragedy was so high, that people rushed out to buy television sets so they could watch at home. (H-E)

THIS HUGE, SEVEN-LAYERED SYMBOLIC cake was decorated with 168 candles in celebration of Los Angeles' 168th birthday in 1949. The candles were lit by civic leaders, who were cheered by a large breakfast crowd in the Biltmore Bowl. Lighting the candles are, left to right, Mrs. Gertrude H. Rounsavelle, Mayor Fletcher Bowron, Mrs. Valley M. Knudsen, and Earle V. Grover, president of the Los Angeles Chamber of Commerce.

FORMAL DANCES, such as this one by the Ebell Juniors in 1949, were common occurrences, as were weddings, bar mitzvahs, dances, parties, fashion shows, and even new automobile exhibits, in the Crystal Room of the Beverly Hills Hotel. The elegant room, which seats five hundred persons for dinner, was opened in 1939, and featured a traditional architecture. Today, it is still as popular as ever, and at times is used by movie studios as a set for films.

THE VENICE BEACH AREA, including adjoining strands of sand at Ocean Park and Santa Monica, became a popular place after World War II at which to engage in or watch sports activities. In those days large crowds gathered for weight lifting, volleyball, bathing beauty contests, gymnastics, and even for boxing and wrestling exhibitions, as this picture shows in 1950. (LADRP)

COULD THIS BE SUNNY CALIFORNIA? One of the coldest nights in Southern California history turned this pair of "longie" pajamas into an icicle man on the clothesline at the home of Mrs. Hortense White of Arcadia in 1949. Icicles also hung from the line, and ice covered the ground. (H-E)

SMUDGE POTS WERE lit by citrus fruit growers when the temperature dropped below freezing near Covina in 1949. The lowest temperatures in Southern California history forced the fruit growers to keep pots firing overnight and long into the next day in an effort to save their fruit. Unofficial temperatures hit 22 degrees in this area. (H-E)

[202]

STREETCARS AND BUSES disappeared from the streets in June of 1950 when a transit workers strike crippled the city. As a result, thousands of persons were forced to use the automobile to get to work. This traffic jam occurred during the evening rush hour at Hill Street, looking east on First. (H-E)

HOLLYWOOD BOULEVARD AND VINE STREET to the whole world was a symbol of the movie industry for a great many years, and even today is still well known to movie fans. But to residents of Hollywood and Los Angeles, it was just like any other intersection around 1950. In those years, the four corners were the home of a department store, a drugstore, a luggage shop, and a restaurant. Looking east on Hollywood, on the left near the corner, is the famous Pantages Theater, where many film premieres were held. (H-E)

Bibliography

Carr, Henry. *Los Angeles, City of Dreams.* New York: D. Appleton-Century Company, 1935.

Coote, James. *A Picture History Of the Olympics.* New York: Macmillan Co., 1972.

Donin, Hayim Halevy. *To Be A Jew.* New York: Basic Books, 1972.

Hendrickson, Joe. *The Tournament of Roses.* Northridge, California: Brooke House, 1971.

McGroarty, John Steven. *California Of the South.* Vol. 1, Los Angeles: S. J. Clarke Publishing Co., 1933

Nadeau, Remi. *Los Angeles, From Mission to Modern City.* New York: Longmans, Green & Co., 1960.

Newmark, Harris. *Sixty Years In Southern California, 1853-1913.* Boston: Houghton Mifflin Co., 1930.

Spalding, William A. *History and Reminiscences, Los Angeles City and County.* Los Angeles: J. R. Finnell & Sons, 1933.

Los Angeles County, Street Atlas, 1973. Los Angeles: Thomas Bros.

Weaver, John D. *El Pueblo Grande.* Pasadena: Ward Ritchie Press, 1973.

Workman, Boyle. *The City That Grew.* Los Angeles: Southland Publishing Co., 1935.

Index of Names